# THE GOOD LIFE IN THE LAST DAYS

## MAKING CHOICES WHEN THE TIME IS SHORT

## MIKEY LYNCH

### FOREWORD BY STEVE TIMMIS

matthiasmedia

SYDNEY · YOUNGSTOWN

*For Nikki*
We were writing this book with our lives
before I began writing it with my keyboard.
Your wisdom and compassion have helped me
learn these things; your patience and
forgiveness have borne with me as I am a
slow learner.

# ACKNOWLEDGEMENTS

Nikki, Xavier, Esther and Toby for their support and love during the whole process.

Luke Isham and Joe Towns for the persistent and enthusiastic encouragement that gave me the confidence boost to have a go at writing a book.

Nikki Lynch, Dan Godden, Renae Godden, Paul Grimmond, Cathie Heard, Luke Isham, Rory Shiner and Dani Treweek for taking the time to read my draft and give insightful feedback.

AFES for granting me a sabbatical to actually get the book written and the AFES Hobart staff and student leadership for cheerfully and capably carrying on in my absence.

Simon and Rebecca for their generous hospitality in giving the Lynch family a writer's retreat.

Matthias Media for accepting this proposal from a first-time author and giving such good vibes alongside great constructive editorial input from Tony Payne and Samantha Dunn.

To the people and communities that have shaped my mind and life, including: David Jones, Pete and Anne Woodcock, Phil Dowe and Jo Kelder in my early years as a

Christian at St John's Presbyterian; my home church for the past 18 years, Crossroads Presbyterian; The Vision 100 Network of Tasmanian churches; the students and alumni of AFES Hobart; the Geneva Push board, staff and church planters; and, of course, my mum and dad for their love and wisdom in raising me.

# CONTENTS

# FOREWORD

A question which has exercised me over the past few years is how do we, as the people God has chosen not only to reveal his glory to, but also to display his glory through, *"proclaim the excellencies of him who called us out of darkness and into his marvellous light"*? God's word is crystal clear that we have been blessed to be a blessing. We have been mandated to carry the good news of all he has done for us in Christ and all that he has for us in Christ to the ends of the earth before he returns to make all things new. But just how do we *do* it? In the everyday circumstances of life, the highs, the lows and the mundane, how do we live as the people we *are* in Christ and as communities of light in the midst of communities of darkness?

It is a self-evident truth that the expectations of our culture shape our discipleship. It seems to me that the pressure on this generation is even more intense than when I was in my prime. Our culture tells us to expect happiness and fulfilment, so we shy away from sacrifice. Our culture tells us that this world is all there is, so we desperately scramble after every satisfying experience we think we need in the here and now. Such idolatry leads to a church that is weakened by distraction, wooed by pleasure and seduced by the mythical allure of autonomy. It leads to a church that is not only ineffective, but also joyless. Like CS Lewis's famous illustration of the ignorant child who turns down a seaside holiday in order to make mud-pies in the slum, we are also far too easily pleased.

In this penetrating book, Mikey offers a biblically informed corrective to our bleak tendency to bow to prevailing assumptions. It calls out the sin of idolatry for sure, but it also brightly communicates the joy and satisfaction that comes with loving God and delighting in God's love—satisfaction that increases and endures. It tackles the paradoxical nature of God's word—on one hand, sacrifice, on the other, enjoyment of his many gifts. It identifies unbiblical extremes and embraces godly zeal.

It is also particularly insightful in the way it combats intensity. Yes—we are disciples of the Servant King and we are called to follow him in sacrifice and suffering. Yes—we are called to make all sorts of decisions with gospel-focussed intentionality, from the career we select to the hobby we pursue. Yes—we say 'no' to good things in life for the better good of following Christ's commission and proclaiming his name. But in the midst of these choices and sacrifices… we laugh. We joke with colleagues. We relish a piece of warm toast with salted butter. We talk late into the night. We share our home with friends. We wrestle with our kids and grandkids. We enjoy our marriages.

Life is complicated. But rather than bemoan that truth, Mikey encourages us to revel in it. God has created this diverse world. The fact that there are always multiple options is not a curse—rather, it provides the blessed humiliation of acknowledging that we cannot do it all. The fact that when we say 'yes' to one thing we are saying 'no' to something else need not be a burden—rather, it provides the deep-breath inducing peace of recognizing our creatureliness.

This is Mikey's first book. I very much hope it won't be his last. It is accessible and profound. Light and perceptive. My prayer is that the Lord will use this book both as a challenging call to sacrifice in the last days, and a deep, refreshing drink of the cool, sparkling water of the freedom that is ours in Christ.

**Steve Timmis**
**CEO, Acts 29**

# PREFACE: WHY READ THIS BOOK?

It's hard to live the Christian life. You have to continually put to death your sinful nature and turn aside from a comfortable life in this world. You have to live in a way that is different than your neighbours, because you are living in the light of eternity. But the Christian life can be hard for us in ways it doesn't need to be, because we can distort the teaching of Scripture so that it smothers us. Christians can get extremely tangled up and discouraged by their idea of what it should mean for them to live the 'full-on Christian life'. A lot of energy goes into worrying about whether we are being zealous enough, or making sure that others are being zealous enough. It seems to me that this worry creates more friction than it does action. This book seeks to show a way forward.

*Have you tried to zealously serve the Lord and hit the wall?* Do you feel like a bruised reed? Maybe it's hard to listen to sermons about the call to lay down your life for the gospel, because it feels so unliveable now. But perhaps your vision of what the Christian life must look like has gone beyond what the Bible is actually teaching? Perhaps there is a better way to think about zeal and sacrifice?

*Are you living the sacrificial Christian life and wondering why so few are keeping up?* Those of us who are strong and sacrificial need to be careful that we don't expect more of our fellow Christians than God does. Who knows? There might be a season of life where we will need to expect less of ourselves, as well.

*Do you regularly give spiritual advice to others?* We who are preachers, teachers and friends, need to know what the Bible commands every Christian to do, what it encourages us to do and what it gives us freedom to choose. If we are not careful, our well-intentioned exhortations and advice can slide into legalism.

*Do you have the sneaking suspicion that you are not a Real Christian?* Many of us can feel confused and deflated about our lives, because we fear that we have sold out. We have made decisions to live a sensible and sustainable life, but how do we know if this is simply worldly compromise?

Probably you are a mix of several of these put together. Whoever you are, I want to help you better understand that the complexity of the world is God's design, and that each Christian is given freedom to obey God according to their particular situation. I am convinced that when you see things this way, you can discover a joyful wisdom that guides you as you sacrificially serve the Lord. In this book, I zoom in to the hard sayings of Jesus and the apostles to understand what they actually mean and zoom out to consider the full counsel of God on how we live the good life in the last days: how we make choices when the time is short.

# INTRODUCTION

**Ruining your life for the greater good**

We can do some of the worst things in the name of the greatest causes. With a genuine desire to live for God and to love a lost world we can hurt those closest to us. Who hasn't met someone who has become hostile to Christianity after growing up in a ministry or missionary family? They felt like their parents loved the congregation more than them. Who hasn't known a faithful, hardworking Christian who reached the point of burnout and never returned to their former zeal? Sadly, the more that worldly ministry ambition and other sinful desires get added to the mix, the more damage is done.

And yet the Lord Jesus calls us:

> "Whoever wants to be my disciple must deny themselves and take up their cross and follow me. For whoever wants to save their life will lose it, but whoever loses their life for me and for the gospel will save it." (Mark 8:34-35)

In the first season of *The West Wing* we watch the breakdown of the marriage of the White House Chief of Staff, Leo

McGarry. After several broken promises Leo comes home late on the night of his wedding anniversary to find his wife, Jenny, standing in the hallway, her bags packed:

Jenny: I can't do this any more. This is crazy. I don't want to live like this. I just can't.

Leo: I'm sorry about the anniversary. I just…

Jenny: It's not the anniversary. It's everything. The whole thing.

Leo: This is the most important thing I'll ever do. I have to do it well.

Jenny: It's not more important than your marriage.

Leo: It *is* more important than my marriage. Right now. These few years while I'm doing this, yes, it is more important than my marriage.[1]

"It is more important than my marriage." That seems an outrageous statement! Of course she should leave him! How could he think, let alone say, such a thing? Yet isn't it tragically true that this exact conversation happens in Christian ministry homes? Although, rather than leaving, a wife may well stay in miserable silence, committed as she is to marriage for life.

But wait. Let's think about this for a second. Technically speaking, is Leo wrong? In the big scheme of things, surely being Chief of Staff to the President of the United States of

1    Lawrence O'Connell Jnr and Patrick Caddell, 'Five Votes Down', *West Wing Transcripts*, episode 1. 4, 13 October 1999 (viewed 1 November 2017): www.westwingtranscripts.com/search.php?flag=getTranscript&id=4

America is actually more important than a single marriage? So much good can be effected for so many millions of people through a noble and competent government. Is Leo right—is this more important than his marriage?

How much more for those doing Christian things? For the apostle Paul exhorts us, "...the time is short. From now on those who have wives should live as if they do not" (1 Cor 7:29). Isn't the eternal good of salvation for others greater than the temporary good of marital happiness? I recoil strongly at the extreme wording of a passage like this—for I really love my wife and want to care for her well—but is it saying something hard but true? It's difficult, isn't it?

If you've ever read Charles Dickens' *Bleak House,* you would recognize the same kind of thing in the character of Mrs Jellyby—so absorbed in her good deeds for the good natives of Borrioboola-Gha that her children go about in rags. We hear stories from the history books and anecdotes from our own friends and acquaintances, of overworked and emotionally absent men and women, sold out for the cause of their career, their politics, their charity, their ministry.

We rightly dread being that guy. Sermons and Christian marriage seminars might even warn against being that girl. And yet doesn't Jesus say, "If anyone comes to me and does not hate father and mother, wife and children, brothers and sisters—yes, even their own life—such a person cannot be my disciple" (Luke 14:26)? How do we put these two things together? After all, Christians are not utilitarians—just because something is hard and painful and costly doesn't mean it's wrong. Just because something may have negative consequences doesn't mean it's wrong.

## From zealous to wise; from radical to sustainable

A pretty common experience for a young convert is to start their Christian life with a period of intense zeal; to be passionate, sacrificial, extreme, unbalanced, reckless. But over time they realize that this can't be sustained. They realize that some of this intensity was naïve and idealistic. And so they begin to slow down and balance out. And perhaps this is a right and realistic approach. The cause of Christian mission is not simply the emergency response to a short-term crisis—it's a long-term relief effort. It's more like long-term chemo than emergency surgery.

And this is good and right, theologically speaking. The New Testament doesn't paint a simple picture of reckless, radical mayhem. Much of 1 Timothy and Titus stand out in this regard. Written towards the end of the apostolic period, these ministry letters give guidance on how to ensure the long-term stability of the church and the gospel mission. Consider for example 1 Timothy 2:1-2:

> I urge, then, first of all, that petitions, prayers, intercession and thanksgiving be made for all people—for kings and all those in authority, that we may live peaceful and quiet lives in all godliness and holiness.

"Peaceful, quiet lives." That sounds a lot less exciting and urgent—positively boring, even. And this is not even restricted to the later books of the New Testament, as though things were cooling off and slowing down at that point in history. Consider this section from 1 Thessalonians, one of the earliest letters in the New Testament:



THE GOOD LIFE IN THE LAST DAYS

...make it your ambition to lead a quiet life: You
should mind your own business and work with your
hands, just as we told you, so that your daily life may
win the respect of outsiders and so that you will not
be dependent on anybody. (1 Thess 4:11-12)

The same passionate, zealous, sacrificial apostle Paul who
wrote "the time is short. From now on those who have wives
should live as if they do not" (1 Cor 7:29), also urged his disciples to "settle down" and lead "quiet lives". The picture of a
godly life is a bit more complex than we might first think.

What about the book of Acts? Surely there we find the
rapid and radical expansion of the church as the word of the
Lord grows and many are added to their number? Yes and
no. Often we miss the timescale of the narrative, because the
story itself is so exciting. Let me give you just two examples
from Paul's letter to the Galatians. First, in Galatians 1:15-18
we learn that somewhere in Acts 9, soon after Paul's conver-
sion, a period of three years elapses during which time he
goes to Arabia and Damascus. Second, in Galatians 2:1 we
discover that between Acts 9-11 (or possibly chapter 15)
another 14 years elapses. The story of Acts is still wonderful,
but it is not as fast-paced as we might think.

It seems to me that some of our zeal comes not so much
from direct scriptural warrant as from imaginative thought
experiments used by preachers as inspirations, as they
describe burning houses, miracle vaccines or shipwrecks.
Even the intense contemplation of the state of the lost can be
a more dominant emphasis in sermons and missionary
appeals than in the balance of Scripture. "If we *really* believed
in the truths of the gospel, what would we do?" we are asked.

But we don't need to *imagine* what we would do. Rather we need to listen to what God instructs us to do in his word. As John Dickson describes:

> The problem is: God's Word does not quite put it that way, and attempts to argue otherwise usually involve stretching biblical passages beyond their plain meaning… as with many other issues, a worthy goal does not grant permission to handle the Scriptures poorly. We are involved in *God's* mission; we must allow his Word to shape our involvement.[2]

There are also important theological truths that inform the choices we make in our lives and our ministries. For example, we need to remember that our redeemer is also our creator; that our Saviour took on a fully human nature in his incarnation and rose again in a resurrected human body. And because of this, the gospel hope is not simply a 'saved soul' but a resurrected and glorified body in the new creation. Christian spirituality is not opposed to life in this world or the pleasures to be had here. It is neither gnostic[3] or ascetic.[4] Our spirituality delights in God the Father and all his words and works: his character, his good creation, his laws and promises, his righteous judgement, his work of salvation and the fulfilment of all things when Christ returns.

---

**2**    John Dickson, *Promoting the Gospel: A Practical Guide to the Biblical Art of Sharing Your Faith,* Blue Bottle Books, Sydney South, 2005, p. 15.
**3**    The name for a collection of 2nd-century beliefs that say the physical world is evil and secret saving knowledge gives us spiritual salvation from it.
**4**    Religious practices that seek to attain godliness through denying physical pleasure.

And this brings a whole bunch of competing values and duties. We are called to delight in the Lord, commanded to fulfil our duties as image-bearers of God in his world, as loving neighbours, dutiful citizens and tender, caring family members. Remember Jesus' rebuke of the Pharisees for setting aside the word of God about honouring your parents, for the sake of their Corban traditions?

> Jesus replied, "And why do you break the command of God for the sake of your tradition? For God said, 'Honour your father and mother', and 'Anyone who curses their father or mother is to be put to death.' But you say that if anyone declares that what might have been used to help their father or mother is 'devoted to God', they are not to 'honour their father or mother' with it. Thus you nullify the word of God for the sake of your tradition." (Matt 15:3-6)

Zeal shouldn't come at the expense of love. Our intensity and urgency can mean that we treat people poorly: we are pushy with those we minister to and inconsiderate of those closest to us. But this is not how we are to live, on the contrary, we must fulfil the Great Commission in a way that still obeys the Greatest Commandments. We must beware of seeking to be devoted to God in a way that neglects our friends and family. The same Paul who wrote "the time is short. From now on those who have wives should live as if they do not" also wrote "Husbands, love your wives, just as Christ loved the church and gave himself up for her... in this same way, husbands ought to love their wives as their own bodies" (Eph 5:25, 28) and "urge the younger women to love their husbands and children... so that no-one will malign the word of God" (Titus 2:4-5). There is much to be said for a biblically obedient concern not to ruin our lives for the glory of God. Our missionary zeal ought to be informed by godly wisdom and loving care. And yet is it possible to over-correct?

## What place, then, for sacrifice?

The stories we hear of neglect and burnout can lead us to over-react against sacrifice. Even our own personal experience can lead us to become wary of radical zeal. We can become ever so careful about 'work-life balance' and so keenly attentive to the needs of our family that we resist any decision or commitment that might have a negative effect upon the health or happiness of ourselves or our family. And in doing so we end up effectively ripping bits out of our Bible:

> "Whoever wants to be my disciple must deny themselves and take up their cross and follow me. For whoever wants to save their life will lose it, but whoever loses their life for me and for the gospel will save it." (Mark 8:34-35)

> "If anyone comes to me and does not hate father and mother, wife and children, brothers and sisters—yes, even their own life—such a person cannot be my disciple." (Luke 14:26)

> The time is short. From now on those who have wives should live as if they do not; those who mourn, as if they did not; those who are happy, as if they were not;

　　　　　THE GOOD LIFE IN THE LAST DAYS

those who buy something, as if it were not theirs to
keep; those who use the things of the world, as if not
engrossed in them. For this world in its present form
is passing away. (1 Cor 7:29-31)

These verses have to mean *something*. Our decisions,
commitments and lifestyles must surely look different if we
are to follow God's word in these areas.

In this book I want to show that there is a *right way* to
sacrifice. It need not be a brute choice between selfish, work-
life preciousness on the one hand and a neglectful, destructive
sacrifice on the other. There is a way of putting these things
together that, even if it's not simple or comfortable, is
nevertheless *good and loving*. A way of living the Christian
life that even if it's not always exciting nor necessarily
painful, is nevertheless *lived in the light of the reality* of Christ's
saving work.

Far from having to strike some kind of balance or
compromise between living in God's good creation and
sacrificing for the gospel in these last days, I want to show
that *sacrificing for the gospel is how to live well in God's good-
but-fallen-creation in these last days*.

And far from being stuck depending on guilt or intuition
to guide us, it is *spiritual reflection upon ourselves and our
circumstances that helps us make decisions within the broad
boundaries of Christian freedom*: there are a variety of ways to
express this sacrificial calling.

**1**

# DEVOTION AND DIVERSITY

There is a tension for Christians between living life and dying to self. We hear the New Testament call to take up our cross daily and follow Jesus, dying to ourselves for the cause of his gospel. But we recognize intuitively that there are many practical duties and needs we all have in order to live well in all the relationships God has placed us in. Should we nobly burn out ourselves, our relationships, our world, for the cause of gospel proclamation? Should we feel guilty for any creature comfort as a worldly weakness? And if not, why not? And if the answer is somewhere in between, how do we figure out where that is?

First, I want us to take a step back from thinking explicitly about the second coming of Christ, gospel preaching and martyrdom. Because in the first place, some of the difficulties we feel about competing moral priorities are a result of living in the created world. And if we don't get our thinking straight about living godly lives as created beings in a vast and complex creation first, we run into all sorts of trouble. Our faith, our thoughts and lives, and ultimately our ministry must delight in the fact that our Father God created things other than himself.

## There are lots of different types of things in the world

An obvious statement if ever there was one! There *are* lots of different types of things in the world: physical things like trees and mountains, living creatures like ants and elephants, human beings whether strangers or friends, inner experiences like thoughts and feelings, potential activities like growing wheat or painting a masterpiece and spiritual things like God and his angels. The world is full and complex.

This simple fact has caused profound spiritual and philosophical difficulties for human beings through the millennia. As we deliberate about all the possible things we could think and do, these various things compete for our attention, our time, our energy. The modern time management saying reminds us that "When you say Yes to something you are saying No to something else". And so when I spend time sleeping, I am not gardening; when I spend time gardening, I am not parenting; when I spend time parenting I am not praying. How do I apportion my time and energy? When I care for my own children, providing a safe and nurturing childhood, I am distracted from providing basic food and emotional support to the impoverished orphan down the road. How do I weigh my moral obligations? Every moment I spend in prayer and Bible reading could also be spent in building up the church of God, but then again perhaps I should be out looking for opportunities to share the gospel with a dying world? What is the correct pattern of the Christian life?

So many of the big issues we wrestle with about how to live our lives are a result of there being lots of different things in the world:

- Career vs family
- Work vs recreation
- Arts and education funding vs charity and health funding
- Marriage for love vs marriage for procreation

And likewise, so many of the issues we wrestle with as Christians in particular are a result of the very same diversity:

- Paid gospel leadership vs godly secular employment
- 'Vine' work vs 'trellis' work in Christian ministry[5]
- Evangelism vs being a good friend
- Mission work vs social work
- Church vs state
- Plain proclamation vs cultural engagement

There are lots of different types of things in the world. And this makes living life a complicated business.

---

5    From the book *The Trellis and the Vine* by Colin Marshall and Tony Payne (Matthias Media, Sydney, 2009). The book uses the metaphor of gardening to describe Christian ministry, where the 'trellis' is the structures of church life that facilitate the growth of the 'vine' of Christian disciples. The book cautions against spending so much time on the work of building the trellis that we don't end up spending much time on growing disciples.

## False starts: trying to simplify things

Most of us have been tempted at one time or another to try to figure this all out by radically simplifying. We think if we can find one straight path through all the complexity, life will be clear and simple. Not only do individual people do this but many of the great religions and philosophies of the world express various attempts to figure these things out by simplifying the world.

*A first attempt is to decide that some of the things in the world basically don't matter at all.* That definitely simplifies things, doesn't it? So the super-spiritual might decide that the mundane life of family, work and politics are not important; the true Good Life consists in contemplation, meditation and prayer. This definitely makes for a simpler roadmap for life. However, this short cut is inadequate. First of all, it is morally problematic. We have already considered in the introduction several examples of people who through single-hearted devotion to one good, neglected their duties to those nearest to them as a result.

Moreover, look closely and you will see that the complexities of life can't be avoided. Even the solitary monk has to make decisions about when to sleep and what to eat. Indeed, even their prayer and contemplation needs to be weighed: what part of Scripture to read? Whom to pray for? Also, I suspect that every single purist has their little quirks, habits and simple pleasures which betray their idealism: they like to think that they do nothing but pray and contemplate Scripture, except that they really love tile mosaics and bird watching as well. Such attempts at simplicity are artificial and so the end result is inconsistent, if not hypocritical. And a similar thing happens when we pour almost all our energy into any other single area: family, art, work, politics, environment, pleasure.

*Another attempt to simplify things says, 'It is all impossibly complex, so it's all relative'.* You could decide perhaps to just follow your heart, or just resign yourself to whatever is before you. There is something humble and realistic in this approach. We can't be everywhere at once. We can't do everything. But behind this humility can be a kind of moral cowardice. Is there no place for radical, principled change? Doing something not because you want to, not because it 'just so happened', but out of rational reflection and subsequent conviction? I know of people who have made significant lifestyle decisions regarding romantic relationships and career paths based on this kind of careful evaluation. They made a radical break with their previous circumstances and natural intuition. Isn't that a good thing too?

*Thirdly, sometimes we seek to create a hierarchy of obligation, so that we can even things out.* One such hierarchy commonplace in Christian circles in the recent past is: Put God first, your spouse (if you have one) second, your children (if you have them) third, your work last. A simple order of value must surely direct our activity, right?

Well, possibly not. Craig Hamilton points out in his book *Wisdom in Leadership* that such priority lists don't clearly map onto real life:

> Do you really only ever see your friends when there's absolutely no possibility you could spend time investing in your family? Do you really only go to work when there's no way for you to spend time with either your family or your friends?

Or is it just whenever there's a clash you choose your family or friends over the work you do at church? But is that really the case? Or are you sometimes away at a conference while some of your friends are seeing a movie?

…there will still be times when you won't answer a phone call or reply to an email because you're sitting around the table having dinner with friends.[6]

There's no obvious way to measure this kind of hierarchy of priorities and there's always more we could do for any of them.

So then, what is a better approach?

## God purposefully created things other than himself

Let's go back to that primitive truth of our Bible—the true and living God is the creator God and he made a real world that is distinct from himself: "In the beginning God created the heavens and the earth… God saw all that he had made, and it was very good" (Gen 1:1, 31). Psalm 24 proclaims: "The earth is the LORD's and everything in it, the world, and all who live in it" (v. 1). And the apostle Paul can remind us, "everything God created is good, and nothing is to be rejected if it is received with thanksgiving, because it is consecrated by the word of God and prayer" (1 Tim 4:4-5).

There are two types of things in existence: God and

6   Craig Hamilton, *Wisdom in Leadership: The How and Why of Leading the People You Serve,* Matthias Media, Sydney, 2015, p. 95.

                            THE GOOD LIFE IN THE LAST DAYS

everything else. And everything else that exists, exists by the decree of God. God chose to create this rich and complicated world. The simple fact that diversity is God's doing should stop us thinking that competing priorities are a problem and warn us against over-simplifying.

Not only did God purposefully create this complex world, he made us creatures with physical needs, emotional yearnings and a whole range of responsibilities.[7] God made us so that many of our needs would be met not directly by him, but as Joe Rigney says, "God has designed us so that *he* would meet some of our needs *through other people*".[8] He could have only made angels who don't marry, and presumably don't need to eat and sleep, but can contemplate and praise continually, but he didn't. Even before the Fall of Adam and Eve, in the Garden of Eden, the image bearers of God were to spend much time and energy on gardening, eating, sleeping, marriage, child-rearing and probably much else besides. Rigney writes:

> Our existence in time, space, and bodies is not a bug; it's a feature, designed by infinite wisdom for the communication of the unfathomable riches of his glory.[9]

---

7    "God's creative deed has involved the making, not merely of *one* other than himself... but of many. He has made a multitude of kinds... he has brought into being those who will have fellowship, not only... with himself, but... with each other. It is important to stress that plurality is not a state of fallenness, from which mankind must return into an undivided unity... He did not make Adam alone at the beginning, and he will not leave him to be alone at the end" (Oliver O'Donovan, *Resurrection and Moral Order: An Outline for Evangelical Ethics,* Apollos, Leicester, 1994, p. 230).

8    Joe Rigney, *The Things of Earth: Treasuring God by Enjoying His Gifts,* Crossway, Wheaton, IL, 2015, p. 81.

9    Rigney, *The Things of Earth,* p. 79. Rigney quotes Peter Leithart who says Christianity is not a "tragic" philosophy: "Within the category of 'tragic metaphysics'... I also include philosophies that treat finitude, temporality, bodiliness, and limitation as philosophical and practical *problems* that must either be transcended or grudgingly accepted" (p. 80).

The divine speeches at the end of the book of Job speak at length about the vastness and strangeness of the world. The gritty wisdom of Ecclesiastes still acknowledges the many simple pleasures of friendship, work, love, wine, sunlight and clothing as good gifts from God.

Lives full of competing priorities and divided attention were part of God's good design.[10] We don't "lose ourselves in God"—as if the ideal state is to melt ourselves and everything else back into God, so that we lose our separate, distinct individuality. Rather we *find* ourselves in God, as Jesus says, "whoever loses their life for me and for the gospel will *save* it" (Mark 8:35). Christ's salvation does not extract us from the physical world, rather:

> Since the children have flesh and blood, he too shared in their humanity so that by his death he might break the power of him who holds the power of death—that is, the devil—and free those who all their lives were held in slavery by their fear of death… For this reason he had to be made like them, fully human in every way, in order that he might become a merciful and faithful high priest in service to God, and that he might make atonement for the sins of the people. (Heb 2:14-15, 17)

The final goal of our salvation is transformed hearts in resurrected bodies living in a new creation.

A constant danger for us, if we want to give God the glory he deserves, is to lose sight of the realness and otherness of

---

10   Michael Hill, *The How and Why of Love: An Introduction to Evangelical Ethics,* Matthias Media, Sydney, 2002. The world is complex in the sense of "composite" (p. 129) but all the different parts have an overall harmony of purpose (p. 71).

the created world. We should have a high regard for God, but we need to be careful that this doesn't lead us to denying that the created world exists as a thing distinct from God. The world is not simply an extension of God, oozing out from him. Michael Wittmer writes:

> Creation may be relative, but it is real. A ham sandwich does provide a window through which we enjoy God—the ultimate end of all things—but it's also a sandwich that we can enjoy for its own sake. Sometimes a sandwich is (mostly) just a sandwich… [Focussing entirely on his gifts] ignores the *God* who gives, [focussing entirely on the giver] refuses to let him be the God *who gives*.[11]

This means that, at least in principle, there doesn't need to be a conflict between fearing God and honouring Caesar, following Christ and honouring your father and mother, dying to self and finding yourself, fishing for fish and fishing for people. We don't entirely 'leave everything to serve God'—as if the ideal life is one which is as close to angelic as possible. Rather we also serve God *in* the other duties and joys he has given us to be occupied with. Joe Rigney writes:

> What does full and supreme love for God look like when it meets one of his gifts? Glad reception and enjoyment of his gifts. Delight in Eve is what full and supreme love for God looks like when it meets Eve.

---

11  Michael E Wittmer, *Becoming Worldly Saints: Can You Serve Jesus and Still Enjoy Your Life?*, Zondervan, Grand Rapids, MI, 2015, p. 65. Wittmer says this tendency is in the work of Jonathan Edwards (p. 66). Through Edwards' influence, I detected the same tendency is present in Rigney's *The Things of Earth.*

Grateful enjoyment of fish tacos is what supreme love for God looks like when it eats fish tacos. Robust pleasure in church softball is what supreme love for God looks like when it plays church softball. Delight in people and love for people is what supreme and full love for God looks like when it meets people.[12]

But this doesn't mean there are no wrong ways of living life. We can navigate these created complexities foolishly or sinfully. The wise, godly path involves:
- putting God before all, above all, in the middle of all and as the end of all (the rest of this chapter) and
- treating each thing and loving each person in the light of what, where and when they are, in the light of what, where and when we are (we will look at this in the next chapter).

## Put God before all, above all and in the middle of all

Hearing that Jesus had silenced the Sadducees, the Pharisees got together. One of them, an expert in the law, tested him with this question: "Teacher, which is the greatest commandment in the Law?"

Jesus replied: "'Love the Lord your God with all your heart and with all your soul and with all your mind'. This is the first and greatest commandment." (Matt 22:34-38)

12 Rigney, *The Things of Earth,* p. 91.

 THE GOOD LIFE IN THE LAST DAYS

Worship is the greatest duty of all. If in theory we got everything else in life 'right' but failed to love the Lord our God, we would have gotten everything wrong. But also, as we'll see, if we get this right then many other things fall into place.

There are a range of metaphors we use to describe this, each with a slightly different shade of meaning. I have grouped them into four: looking first at the foundational importance of our love for God, then at where he stands in the hierarchy of all we love, thirdly at the centrality of this love and finally at the purpose of our love for God.[13]

## 1. Love God before all things

God comes first, before other things. Historically he came first in time, indeed he is before time itself. Without him there would have been nothing, without him everything would cease:

> Rather, he himself gives everyone life and breath and everything else… For in him we live and move and have our being. (Acts 17:25b, 28a)

> For from him and through him and for him are all things.
> To him be the glory forever! Amen. (Rom 11:36)

Historically he came first, and personally he comes first, too. We only live because he graciously gave us life. And our

---

13  To summarize: Sequence (before/first/foundational), hierarchy (above/highest/supreme), centrality (core/key) and end (goal/purpose).

primary relationship and foundational calling is to know him and worship him. This is why God's word can often speak in sharp black-and-white categories: either you are in Christ or in Adam, sons of God or sons of the Devil, in the flesh or in the Spirit, of the light or of the darkness.[14] And this truth is even starker for us as condemned sinners. For without repentance and faith in response to the gospel, we all stand condemned. Before anything else we must repent and believe the good news. But this good news is available to us because God himself took the initiative to send Christ into the world to forgive our sins and give us new life in him by faith— even in salvation, God comes first.

God comes first in history, first in our personal lives and first in our moral actions as well. Trusting, loving and obeying God is foundational, primal, fundamental to our moral lives:

> The fear of the LORD is the beginning of knowledge. (Prov 1:7)

> …everything that does not come from faith is sin. (Rom 14:23)

> And without faith it is impossible to please God, because anyone who comes to him must believe that he exists and that he rewards those who earnestly seek him. (Heb 11:6)

Once we do believe, not only are our sins pardoned, not only is Christ's righteousness credited to us, but even our imperfect good deeds are acceptable to God in Christ by the Spirit. Have you turned from sin, the world, the flesh and

---

14  O'Donovan, *Resurrection and Moral Order,* p. 260.

   THE GOOD LIFE IN THE LAST DAYS

the devil? Have you given up trusting in frail human effort
and instead put your full confidence in Christ's atoning
death and vindicating resurrection? In order for our lives to
be pleasing to God we must be in Christ, walking by the
Spirit, living by faith.

## 2. Love God above all things

God is before all things and he is also above all things, he is
God of gods, Lord of lords, King of kings. He is supreme.
This is why the greatest commandment is so universal in its
scope: "Hear, O Israel: The LORD our God, the LORD is one.
Love the LORD your God with all your heart and with all
your soul and with all your strength" (Deut 6:4-5).

There is only one God and creator, and so he is worthy of
all love, honour, glory and praise from every part of every
being. This is one reason hierarchies of priorities break
down, because we can never exhaust our duty towards God.
O'Donovan writes: "This stands as a warning against every
attempt to mark off God's demand… in such a way that it
could be exhaustively met, leaving us free to go on to meet
other demands or to take a rest. God's demand is not one
among others."[15] To fail to love God above all things is the
very heart of sin: the foolish, proud and thankless rebellion
that leads to the worship of false gods and every other kind
of evil (Rom 1:18-32).

The supremacy of God calls for this universal love which
must express its obedience to him in all things, as the
surrounding context of the command of Deuteronomy 6

15  O'Donovan, *Resurrection and Moral Order,* p. 233.

demonstrates: it speaks about dwelling on and talking about God's word in all our everyday tasks. This means that we must never obey any other internal desire or external authority that directly conflicts with God's moral commands. It is better that we suffer for doing good, following the example of Christ himself, as 1 Peter encourages us. In the same way, we must never allow any internal desire or external authority to stop us from following the commands related to God's agenda in salvation history, for example:

> The apostles were brought in and made to appear before the Sanhedrin to be questioned by the high priest. "We gave you strict orders not to teach in this name," he said. "Yet you have filled Jerusalem with your teaching and are determined to make us guilty of this man's blood."
>
> Peter and the other apostles replied: "We must obey God rather than human beings!" (Acts 5:27-29)

There are subtleties here. Many moral commands could have multiple applications. So, for example, the command to replace greed with generosity doesn't come with a dollar amount. A Christian married to a non-Christian cannot simply overrule any disagreement about charitable and church contributions on the basis that God commands generosity. Likewise, the command to preach the gospel does not require a missionary in a 'closed country' to insist on open air preaching. Indeed, often we need to weigh up two commands that both come from God and decide a course of action. Nevertheless these nuances don't undermine that broader principle that God is the supreme authority in every area of our lives, and even areas of complexity must be navigated with the intent to be lovingly obedient to him. This flows nicely into our next point.

## 3. Put the love of God at the centre of all things

The love of God comes first, holds the highest authority and also sits at the centre of all other loves and duties. As we have already been reminded, the book of Proverbs begins with the teaching "The fear of the LORD is the beginning of knowledge" (Prov 1:7) and after teaching about the two greatest commandments, Jesus concludes by telling us that "All the Law and the Prophets hang on these two commandments" (Matt 22:40).

Because this whole world is God's world we will see it rightly when we see it from his perspective. God's word interprets his world. Without his revelation we will not properly understand the order and purpose of the world and of our lives.[16] It is a common idea in the New Testament that a godly and mature faith will equip us with the ability to make wise decisions, for example:

> Therefore, I urge you, brothers and sisters, in view of God's mercy, to offer your bodies as a living sacrifice, holy and pleasing to God—this is your true and proper worship. Do not conform to the pattern of this world, but be transformed by the renewing of your mind. Then you will be able to test and approve what God's will is— his good, pleasing and perfect will. (Rom 12:1-2)

16 Graeme Goldsworthy, 'Gospel and Wisdom' in *The Goldsworthy Trilogy,* Paternoster, Carlisle, 2002, pp. 375-94.

Knowing God and knowing his word helps us know ourselves and know his world. The rest of our lives are ordered around our knowledge of God and love of God. As Augustine wrote in his *Confessions*, "He loves You [God] too little who loves anything together with [at same time as] You, which he loves not for Your sake".[17] You see this assumption at work in the Bible in the various ways in which the character of God or of Christ are used to encourage us to live, and in the many ways in which we are encouraged to reflect on God's work in salvation to inform our values and behaviour. We are to be honest for God is faithful, loving for God is loving, forgiving for in Christ God forgave us, generous to the slave and the stranger because God rescued Israel from slavery in Egypt.[18]

As we put God at the centre of all things, we then learn that we can love and worship him in all the other aspects of our lives: I do not only honour God in my explicitly Godward activities, like prayer and Bible reading, but I also honour him as I obey his word about work and friendship. I honour him by seeing all things as his creation, and doing all things for his glory. Because it is all God's world, not some competing type of existence, it was designed by him so that all of it can be caught up in our worship of him.

This underlines the importance of motivation, as Paul says to the Colossians, "Whatever you do, whether in word or deed, do it all in the name of the Lord Jesus, giving thanks to God the Father through him" (Col 3:17). We should do all that we do in faith and thankfulness. Ultimately it is not

---

17 Augustine, 'The Confessions', book X, chapter 29. Accessed from *New Advent* (viewed 18 October 2017): www.newadvent.org/fathers/110110.htm
18 Andrew Cameron, *Joined-Up Life: A Christian Account of How Ethics Works*, IVP, Nottingham, 2011, pp. 128-34, 143-7.

                     THE GOOD LIFE IN THE LAST DAYS

enough for an action to be objectively and externally moral, the motivation must also be godly. This is not only a challenge, but also a reassurance because it also means that no matter how feeble or unimpressive we are, if we are motivated by the glory of God we are doing something divinely valued. As the 17th-century bishop Joseph Hall crisply summarizes it:

> The homeliest service that we do in an honest calling, though it be but to plough or dig, if done in obedience, and conscience of God's commandment, is crowned with an ample reward; whereas the best works of their kind—preaching, praying, offering evangelical sacrifices—if without respect of God's injunction and glory, are loaded with curses. God loveth adverbs; and cares not how good, but how well.[19]

Our God is the creator who comes before all things, the Lord who rules over all things, the wisdom that gives meaning and purpose to all things and the ultimate goal in whom all things find their fulfilment.

## 4. See loving God as the end goal of all things[20]

This creation is not timeless, nor is it eternal in its current form. It had a beginning, when God spoke it into being, and it will have an end, when Christ returns and God makes a new heavens and a new earth. The Bible repeatedly cele-

---

19  Joseph Hall, 'Holy Observations', in A Huntington Clapp (ed.), *A Selection from the Writings of Joseph Hall,* Allen, Morrill and Wardwell, New York, 1845, p. 149. Accessed from *Google Play* (viewed 18 October 2017): play.google.com/store/books/details?id=f9gTAAAAYAAJ&rdid=book-f9gTAAAAYAAJ&rdot=1
20  Thanks to Tony Payne for suggesting the addition of this final point.

brates that all things come from God, find their being in God and are created for God (Rom 11:36; Col 1:16; Heb 2:10). This is the goal to which all things are heading, as Ephesians describes it:

> With all wisdom and understanding, he made known to us the mystery of his will according to his good pleasure, which he purposed in Christ, to be put into effect when the times reach their fulfilment—to bring unity to all things in heaven and on earth under Christ. (Eph 1:8b-10)

He is not only the beginning but also the end, not only the first but also the last, not only the 'Alpha' but also the 'Omega' (Revelation 1 and 22). In the first place this is another way of thinking about the importance of the glory of God in all things because all things find their ultimate purpose in the glory of God.

Seeing loving God as the end of all things also reminds us that we are still looking ahead to that end. This means that any attempt to find perfection and completion in this age is doomed to frustration or self-deception: "What is crooked cannot be straightened; what is lacking cannot be counted," the Teacher says in Ecclesiastes 1:15 and "If we claim to be without sin, we deceive ourselves and the truth is not in us", John writes in his first letter (1 John 1:8). Human ideologies, whether Christian or non-Christian, often become tyrannical and destructive when they try to achieve perfection in this world: reformers can become cult leaders and revolutionaries can become dictators. Our judgements should always be cautious and provisional in this life, we have not yet arrived— "judge nothing before the appointed time", as the apostle

   THE GOOD LIFE IN THE LAST DAYS

Paul provocatively puts it (1 Cor 4:5).[21]

There is a more positive side to this too: as we love God and our neighbour (more of that in the next chapter), however imperfectly, we are living in the light of the fulfilment of all things. This is why Paul can speak in 1 Corinthians 13 of the greatness of love above the many and various things we might do:

> Love never fails. But where there are prophecies, they will cease; where there are tongues, they will be stilled; where there is knowledge, it will pass away. For we know in part and we prophesy in part, but when completeness comes, what is in part disappears. When I was a child, I talked like a child, I thought like a child, I reasoned like a child. When I became a man, I put the ways of childhood behind me. For now we see only a reflection as in a mirror; then we shall see face to face. Now I know in part; then I shall know fully, even as I am fully known.
>
> And now these three remain: faith, hope and love. But the greatest of these is love. (1 Cor 13:8-13)

To summarize, God intentionally created this complex world so it will not do to seek godliness through oversimplifying. To begin to navigate this world of otherness and diversity we must love God before all things, above all things, at the centre of all things and as the ultimate end of all things.

Like many truths of Scripture this is both challenging and encouraging. It is challenging because it is the highest

---

21   Paul doesn't mean there is no place for judgements at all. In the very next chapter he talks about the need for church discipline. His point is that we must also hold our merely human judgements as imperfect and limited. See also Jesus' parable of the weeds and the wheat (Matt 13:24-30, 36-43).

standard of all. Who of us can truly say that we love God with all our heart and all our mind and all our soul and all our strength? Who of us has not allowed our fear of people, or personal preference or the ease of conformity to divert us from obedience to God's will and purpose? Who of us doesn't have areas of our thinking, feeling, dreaming, planning, budget, calendar and habits untouched by the central concern of worship? What greater challenge is there than this? Thanks be to God for his daily mercy to us in the gospel of Jesus Christ!

But this is also encouraging. It is encouraging simply to recognize that life is complicated and God made it that way. If you find it hard to balance all the various desires, duties, priorities and pressures of life, then there's nothing wrong with you necessarily. God made the world in such a way that sometimes we sleep when we could be praying, we play with our children when we could be evangelizing, we do a crossword when we could be helping the poor. The Bible assumes and teaches that this is the way the created world works. Nothing is ultimately mundane. We can and should worship God in vacuuming the house, playing cricket, cooking falafel, building websites and changing nappies.

It is also encouraging to focus on the formative influence of genuine love of God. We may be overwhelmed by our hectic lives and moral quandaries, but we can take comfort that if we love the Lord we truly will live well in the ways that really matter. As Augustine famously said in his sermon on 1 John 4:4-12: "Love God and do what you will".[22]

---

**22** Augustine, 'Homilies on First Epistle of of John', in Philip Schaff (ed.), *A Select Library of the Nicene and Post-Nicene Fathers of the Christian Church*, vol. VII, T&T Clark, Edinburgh, 1900. Accessed from *Christian Classics Ethereal Library* (viewed 18 October 2017): www.ccel.org/ccel/schaff/npnf107.i.html

**2**

# DEVOTION, DIVERSITY AND THE DAY-TO-DAY

I remember the intense zeal of those first few years after becoming a Christian towards the end of my last year of high school. I can still recall the feeling. The world suddenly grew bigger, like the roof was lifted off: there was a God! A heaven and a hell! There was great delight in learning about Christ and learning to live for him, experiencing Christian community and reading the Bible from beginning to end. There was also great earnest passion to share the gospel with anyone and everyone, especially old friends and family members. The gospel is so good, so true and so urgent! I diligently mapped out my time and worked the phone (a landline back then) to try to connect with family and friends and acquaintances, with a hope that the topic of Christianity might come up.

But sadly this genuine desire can make others feel as if they are 'projects' rather than people—and unfortunately the truth was they sometimes became that in my own heart, too. No doubt many thought I was treating them like a project, and most likely plenty said it, but the ones who really forced me to hear it were my close friends. They said sometimes it seemed like I stopped seeing them as a friend and just saw them as a person going to Hell and they resented it. In my best moments this wasn't my intention but, as I tried to explain to them, I struggled to even understand how I could be a good friend to a non-Christian in a normal, everyday way. That's what the expression 'Bible-bashing' describes. When you are Bible-bashed you are no longer a person someone is having a conversation with. You have been reduced to an object to be bashed. And the Bible is no longer a book to be explained and understood. It has become merely a tool, or weapon, to do the bashing with.

What is the solution to this kind of conflict of priorities? I didn't want to 'bash' anyone but I did want those I loved to seriously consider the claims of Christ. I wanted them to realize how important and time-sensitive this message was. To be silent seemed unconscionable, and even to be too gentle, hesitant and courteous seemed to distort the nature of the message that I was wanting to communicate. It was hard to get this right in my own head and heart, let alone in practice.

Remember Leo McGarry from *The West Wing*? "It is more important than my marriage. Right now. These few years while I'm doing this, yes, it is more important than my marriage." Was he wrong to neglect his marriage for the sake of such a great responsibility? Was it selfish careerism? Or could it have been equally selfish to fixate on his own love life to the detriment of the public service of millions of people?

     THE GOOD LIFE IN THE LAST DAYS

There are many smaller moral problems we encounter every day, too. How to apportion time to immediate family, ageing relatives, work commitments, old friends, new friends, church, parachurch, home improvement, fitness, hobbies? How do I plan my giving—to my local church, to an AFES[23] evangelist, to a developing world charity, to a community radio station?

As we have seen, God made a rich and complex creation, where there are many competing priorities. This isn't a problem with the world, but the Creator's deliberate design. When we put God first the most fundamental things fall into place so that everything else is done trusting in him, in obedience to him, for his glory. But this doesn't mean the rest is easy. For Jesus not only gives us the greatest commandment but also the second greatest commandment:

> Jesus replied: "'Love the Lord your God with all your heart and with all your soul and with all your mind'. This is the first and greatest commandment. And the second is like it: 'Love your neighbour as yourself'." (Matt 22:37-39)

How do we live out lives of love for our neighbour when there are so many neighbours, with so many needs: both short-term and long-term, both personal and global, both temporal and eternal? To answer this question involves a broad study of Christian ethics[24] but below are three

---

23   The Australian Fellowship of Evangelical Students, a ministry to university students. See afes.org.au for more information.

24   Two helpful introductions by Australian authors are: Andrew Cameron's *Joined-Up Life* (IVP, Nottingham, 2011) and Michael Hill's *The How and Why of Love: An Introduction to Evangelical Ethics* (Matthias Media, Sydney, 2002).

principles that capture some key planks of Christian ethics which will be unpacked in the rest of this book:

- Treat each thing and love each person as who they are, where they are and when they are.
- Know who we are, where we are and when we are.
- Understand Christian freedom.

## Treat each thing and love each person as who they are, where they are and when they are

Far from simplifying the world by ignoring other things and other people as distractions, the key to the Christian life is to become more attentive; and to see them rightly. As we see God before, above, at the centre and as the ultimate end of all things, we see the world as he intends it to be—as it truly is. And as we see the world as it was truly created to be, it becomes clearer how to conduct ourselves in it: what to love and what to hate. We need the light of God's word to guide us in deciphering things as they are in themselves, where they are in the world and 'when' they are in time—and what this means for how we should treat them. Sinful desires are disordered desires, which lead us to desire and use things in a manner and to a degree that is against their created nature and purpose. Godly living sees the world rightly and so conforms desires and actions to God's good purposes (Eph 4:17-24).[25]

*Firstly, when we see someone as WHO they are we will be*

---

25  In *Resurrection and Moral Order*, O'Donovan writes: "Love cannot be love in a vacuum of intelligibility; the human soul loves only on the basis of an understanding of its object" (p. 236).

   THE GOOD LIFE IN THE LAST DAYS

*better able to love them appropriately*. Consider the example of 'Bible-bashing'. A non-Christian might call their friend a Bible-basher because they themselves are overly sensitive and defensive about Christianity, possibly because of past hurt or even because of guilt arising from suppressing the truth. Or a Christian might adopt a style of personal interaction that could be described as Bible-bashing because they, wrongly in my view, believe that a kind of ferocious, prophetic earnestness is the appropriate stance a Christian ought to take in personal evangelism. However, I believe we often slip into a Bible-bashing approach when we become too task-oriented, forgetting to treat people as who they are: fellow image bearers, who feel and think, who need to be respected and reasoned with… and also just kindly chatted with about the weather and whether they had smashed avo for breakfast. The AFES Code of Conduct for Staff puts this very well in expressing both a zealous resolve to proclaim Christ alongside "disavow[ing] any approaches which *de-personalise people*" [emphasis mine]:

> [We seek] to honour the Lord through an ethical and open approach in our attempts to persuade others to believe the good news about Jesus Christ.
>
> - We disavow any approaches which de-personalise people; or that seek their conversion through manipulative, coercive, or overly emotional means which bypass a person's critical faculties, or that mask the true nature and demands of Christian conversion.
> - We believe in the gospel of Jesus Christ, and affirm the necessity of the proclamation of Christ to every person. As evangelists, we will pursue this goal with

openness, revealing our identity and purpose, theological positions, and sources of information. We will engage people of other religious persuasions in true dialogue, listening carefully and responding honestly and graciously.

- We will especially have care in our evangelistic relationships with international students. We will be diligent in expressing the welcome of the Lord Jesus to people of all ethnic and linguistic backgrounds, and we disavow any racism. We also understand that some will come from cultural backgrounds where there is high respect for older people and authority figures, and also where there is a sense of obligation to those who provide some service or friendship. For these reasons, international students must be treated carefully to give full expression to the freedom of their response to the Gospel without any (even unintended) coercion.[26]

Indeed our particular relationship with the person—whether friend, boss, stranger, daughter—ought to also affect our approach in personal evangelism. AFES acknowledges this with its third bullet point on the unique relationship with international students (for biblical examples see 1 Tim 5:1 and 1 Pet 3:1-2). We will explore this more when we consider that we should also treat people 'where they are', below.

The same principle of loving people as they are also applies to *treating things as they are*. Sins of excess—like vanity, gluttony, greed and laziness—abuse good things by

26  AFES Code of Conduct for Staff (adopted 1 September 2007), p. 5.

  THE GOOD LIFE IN THE LAST DAYS

loving them too much, in a bloated, uncontrolled manner. In doing so they are not treating them *as they are* in proportion to other good things. Calvin puts his finger on this so well:

> Certainly ivory and gold, and riches, are the good creatures [creations] of God, permitted, nay destined, by divine providence for the use of man; nor was it ever forbidden to laugh, or to be full, or to add new to old and hereditary possessions, or to be delighted with music, or to drink wine. This is true, but when the means are supplied to roll and wallow in luxury, to intoxicate the mind and soul with present and be always hunting after new pleasures, is very far from a legitimate use of the gifts of God. Let them, therefore, suppress immoderate desire, immoderate profusion, vanity, and arrogance, that they may use the gifts of God purely with a pure conscience. When their mind is brought to this state of soberness, they will be able to regulate the legitimate use. On the other hand, when this moderation is wanting, even plebeian and ordinary delicacies are excessive.[27]

*Secondly, we are to treat people WHERE they are*: what is their place in the world and their place in relationship to you? The moral ideal of the 18th-century movement known as the Enlightenment was the ideal of universal benevolence: that we should be motivated by an impartial, universal love for all of humanity, not only in the present but into the

---

**27** John Calvin, *Institutes of the Christian Religion,* trans. Henry Beveridge, Christian Classics Ethereal Library, Grand Rapids, MI, book III, chapter 19, section 9 (viewed 19 October 2017): www.ccel.org/ccel/calvin/institutes

future as well.[28] And this ethical heritage still affects us today, so that we are burdened to feel an equal amount of love for every human being on the planet, and so assume a moral obligation for every human being. In fact, this feeling is probably even stronger now that electronic media and air travel shrink the world to feel like our neighbourhood.

There is indeed a Christian moral truth in this idea: all human beings are made in the image of God, all are equally sinful so there is no difference, God gave his salvation for the world. In this sense, we must not seek to limit the command to love our neighbour by asking "Who is my neighbour?" (Luke 10:29), but rather should seek to *be* a neighbour to all without discrimination (10:36-37). In a similar way, Jesus teaches in the Sermon on the Mount that love must not be restricted only to those who love us in return:

> "You have heard that it was said, 'Love your neighbour and hate your enemy'. But I tell you, love your enemies and pray for those who persecute you, that you may be children of your Father in heaven. He causes his sun to rise on the evil and the good, and sends rain on the righteous and the unrighteous. If you love those who love you, what reward will you get? Are not even the tax collectors doing that? And if you greet only your own people, what are you doing more than others? Do not even pagans do that?" (Matt 5:43-47)

However, undifferentiated, universal love is not only emotionally impossible to feel and physically impossible to

---

28 Charles Taylor, *Sources of the Self: The Making of the Modern Identity*, Cambridge University Press, Cambridge, 1989, pp. 322, 329-31.

  THE GOOD LIFE IN THE LAST DAYS

enact (more of this under the next sub-heading), it is not the unqualified moral teaching of the Bible.[29]

In the Bible, God teaches that we have a range of responsibilities, with something of an order of priorities, with our relatives and immediate family (1 Tim 5:4, 8) and fellow Christians (Gal 6:10) high on the list. The book of Proverbs also speaks highly of 'friendship' as another category like this. Although Jesus taught the parable of the Good Samaritan to warn against a limited definition of 'neighbour' (perhaps based on age, race, religion, class, power, sex, health, looks or moral performance) it remains true that the command does refer to 'neighbour': someone who is close to us in proximity, not simply 'fellow human being'. In fact, the parable itself reinforces this, for the Good Samaritan comes across the man he helps in physical proximity.[30]

Electronic media brings people closer to us so that we can see their plight and air travel brings people closer to us so that we can reach them, and globalisation brings people closer to us so that we can touch them. In that sense it probably is true that more people have become our neighbours, just like moving from an isolated farm to an

---

**29** And possibly not the unqualified moral teaching of Enlightenment Utilitarians either, but this is the moral 'vibe' to be drawn from this heritage.

**30** O'Donovan, *Resurrection and Moral Order*, p. 240. "An ethic of undifferentiated love which allowed of no application to proximate relations could have little relevance for embodied human beings who can be in only one place at a time, and must needs be closer to some people than to others." See also the great discussion of this in Kevin DeYoung and Greg Gilbert, *What is the Mission of the Church? Making Sense of Social Justice, Shalom and the Great Commission,* Crossway, Wheaton, 2011, pp. 183-6 and Rigney, *The Things of Earth,* pp. 207-10.

apartment building.[31] However, while this might create a new category of our 'global village neighbour', it remains true that such 'neighbours' have a different moral demand on us than our physical neighbours.

We are to treat people according to where they are in the world and in relation to us. This is part of where Leo McGarry from *The West Wing* gets it wrong. While objectively he might be right that running a country is more important than being a husband, he is wrong about what that means for his personal conduct: it's not more important than his marriage *for him*. As a prayer letter I received just this week described it: "Home is the first place we're called to display the love of Christ. Our spouse and children are our nearest neighbours."[32] It seems that this TV character has failed to be wise in the way that he manages the pressures of his challenging work

31 Matt Perman, *What's Best Next: How the Gospel Transforms the Way You Get Things Done,* Zondervan, Grand Rapids, MI, 2014. Location 5163–5179. "Technology now enables us to use some of this [free] time and these resources [of affluence] to take large-scale action to address large global problems because it amplifies our ability to connect with others and do good on a larger scale—in many cases without even having to leave our homes… We can loan to entrepreneurs in the developing world from our living rooms in Kiva; we can encourage missionaries halfway around the world within seconds through a quick email; we can purchase wells, medicine, and crops for those in need at the website of Food for the Hungry; we can let hundreds of people know about ways to serve global needs through a quick re-tweet on Twitter; we can expose hundreds of others to a biblical truth through a simple (and tactful) Facebook post or a link to an article." Of course, we need to ask whether forms of good that are convenient to wealthy people in information societies are always actually the most effective in the long-term, and beware hiding behind our screens to do good in ways that are convenient to us, rather than being more 'hands on' and 'face to face' where that might be better. I also don't think Perman structures the relationship of good deeds to gospel mission well in this chapter.

32 The quote was taken from Chap Bettis, 'Home Is the Front Lines of Christian Living', *The Gospel Coalition,* 22 April 2017 (viewed 19 October 2017): www.thegospelcoalition.org/article/home-is-front-lines-of-christian-living

   THE GOOD LIFE IN THE LAST DAYS

life alongside nurturing his love life. This wasn't an impossible challenge, as his boss—the President of the United States—managed to make time for his wife. The importance of one's public life does not overrule the personal duties of one's private life.

*Last of all, we should treat people according to WHEN they are.* What time is it? What circumstances surround this time? A time of illness or a time of honeymoon? Early years of a church plant, raising young children or starting a business? Time is one of the major themes of the book of Ecclesiastes, where it is both a positive and a negative thing. The famous poem of chapter 3 says "There is a time for everything and a season for every activity under the heavens" (v. 1) and even God has "made everything beautiful in its time" (v. 11a). Later on in the book we are told that "there is a proper time and procedure for every matter" (8:6). Negatively, the very same book recognizes that there is much we can't know because "He has also set eternity in the human heart; yet no-one can fathom what God has done from beginning to end" (3:11). The author writes "When times are good, be happy; but when times are bad, consider this: God has made the one as well as the other. Therefore, no-one can discover anything about their future" (7:14) and "the race is not to the swift or the battle to the strong, nor does food come to the wise or wealth to the brilliant or favour to the learned; but time and chance happen to them all" (9:11).

The Old Testament law formalizes times for feasting and for fasting, for working and for resting, and many narratives and parables also reflect similar seasons in the personal lives of God's people. The book of Deuteronomy makes an allowance for the unique 'time' of newly married life: such a couple is given twelve months' reprieve from the husband being called off to war (Deut 20:7, 24:5).[33] At many points in John's gospel Jesus comments on what is and isn't appropriate given the 'time' or 'hour' it is (2:4, 7:6-10, 12:23-36, 16:19-32). It's impossible to write a timetable of the perfectly balanced week and then run that exact timetable every week from now until Christ returns. As the seasons of life shift and change, what we do needs to shift and change.

Craig Hamilton describes this as "situational priorities" and pictures our various relationships and responsibilities as lily pads that shift closer and further away depending upon the situation.[34] Some times might be dictated by external events such as a sudden emergency. But they might also be determined by more predictable forces: our age, the time of day, change of seasons, a special occasion or a duration of activity. In part, it seems this is the failure of our running fictional example from *The West Wing*: he failed to rightly value the importance of the time of his wedding anniversary. More than this, reading between the lines of the dialogue this had been a recurring problem. In the chaos of life, and especially a high-pressured job, it is impossible to always be present for important events. And yet over time a consistent pattern of failure to be proactive and creative in remembering anniversaries, being on time for picking up the kids, keeping holidays uninterrupted and being available in emergencies may well demonstrate a failure to treat others 'according to

33 Christopher Ash points out that this is possibly not so much about spending 'quality time', much less some kind of justification for taking a year off leading youth group when you get married (!). Rather this law was to keep him from dying long enough to start a family! Christopher Ash, *Marriage: Sex in the Service of God*, IVP, Leicester, 2003, p. 162.
34 Hamilton, *Wisdom in Leadership*, pp. 95-7.

          THE GOOD LIFE IN THE LAST DAYS

the times'. And this compounds. Past history gives extra meaning to the present 'times': a failure to remember an anniversary adds additional significance to future failing (or succeeding) to remember.

There are longer seasons of time as well—like terms of military service, off-shore work and touring, to name a few that are the result of careers—which also dramatically influence what behaviour is possible and appropriate. Such seasons become a unique "life package", to use Andrew Cameron's term.[35] I know some retired missionaries who worked in various Pacific Islands while raising a young family, before the husband became a professor of missiology in the United States. When the children were young, tropical diseases were a serious danger. As they grew older they spent much of their lives at missionary boarding school, and as young adults most of them were falling in love, getting married and having children in Australia while their parents were still in the US. Now the missionary couple have returned to Australia, to live close to several of their children and, more importantly, most of their grandchildren! The husband said to me about this season of life: "She followed me on my ministry around the world. Now it's my turn. I'm here for her and for the grandchildren." For some couples a pivot like this so late in life would seem like a poor concession indeed. We could also clarify that even their overseas missionary service was a ministry they shared together, it was not just *his* ministry, which I know was true in their case. Yet for this couple, recognizing this season of retirement as not yet another context for his external ministry responsibilities

35 Cameron, *Joined-Up Life*, pp. 231-2.

to dominate but a season for his ministry to turn towards being present with and for his wife, children and grandchildren's needs, was fitting.

The longest possible time frame is of course your whole life, the second coming and then the resurrection to life or condemnation. How can we not consider these factors in our attitude towards people and things? This perspective will become much more central in the subsequent chapters, as we turn to look at 1 Corinthians 7.[36]

## Know who *we* are, where we are and when we are

To know how to live our lives in a world of competing priorities we need to love people remembering who they are, where they are and when they are. But we also need to know who *we* are, where *we* are and when *we* are.

In his small book *Zeal Without Burnout*, Christopher Ash reminds us that "we are dust": we are frail, limited and mortal. We are not gods. So we need sleep, we need Sabbath rests, we need friends, we need inward renewal.[37] We need to know our physical, emotional, psychological and spiritual limitations. Failure to pay attention to these realities can

---

36 Another instructive example is the story of Jesus' anointing in Matthew 26:6-13. His disciples reasonably argue that the lavish gesture would have been better diverted to help the poor. But Jesus says that the woman who anointed him with perfume did a "beautiful thing to me" (v. 10), which was especially appropriate because of the time: "The poor you will always have with you, but you will not always have me. When she poured this perfume on my body, she did it to prepare me for burial" (vv. 11-12). Since the woman did not have this full knowledge, it seems that her motive of devotion, based on *who* Jesus is was also important.

37 Christopher Ash, *Zeal Without Burnout: Seven Keys to a Lifelong Ministry of Sustainable Sacrifice,* The Good Book Company, UK, 2016.

　THE GOOD LIFE IN THE LAST DAYS

have disastrous results for our wellbeing, our relationships and even our faith. As is often observed, even Jesus in his humanity was limited by his need for food and sleep. Knowing our limitations is different to selfishness, it's a humble recognition of our place in God's world. In my experience it is not easy to trust a person who hasn't yet learned the maturity to say 'No' from time to time, because often they will say 'Yes' when they realistically are unable to fulfil their commitment. Either they will not follow through and let you down, or they will follow through at undue personal cost and resent you for it. A person who has learned the wisdom of the judicious 'No' can be trusted because you know that when they say 'Yes' they are able to do a task reliably and joyfully.

Each of us have varying capacities, influenced by our physical and emotional constitution, as well as all sorts of other factors, including lifelong formative experiences. Knowing ourselves well makes us better able to 'dial in' what we are and are not able to handle. And it should also warn us against being too quick to judge others: we don't know the full story, it's not as simple as saying "if I were in their shoes I would…" In various places the Bible assumes varying degrees of capacity and responsibility. For example, it is noteworthy that in the parable of the bags of gold, each of the servants is entrusted with a different size of responsibility as symbolized by the different sums of gold (Matt 25:14-30). Likewise, in Romans 12 Paul writes:

> For by the grace given me I say to every one of you:
> Do not think of yourself more highly than you ought,
> but rather think of yourself with sober judgement, in
> accordance with the faith God has distributed to each

of you… We have different gifts, according to the grace given to each of us. (vv. 3, 6)

We also need to be aware of 'where' we are: the responsibilities and relationships we're already involved in. As we will explore in detail in later chapters, this is one reason God commends the single life in 1 Corinthians 7. By freeing someone up from the many demanding responsibilities of everyday married and family life, single people are potentially more available for devotional life and missionary endeavour, as Paul writes:

> I would like you to be free from concern. An unmarried man is concerned about the Lord's affairs—how he can please the Lord. But a married man is concerned about the affairs of this world—how he can please his wife—and his interests are divided. An unmarried woman or virgin is concerned about the Lord's affairs: Her aim is to be devoted to the Lord in both body and spirit. But a married woman is concerned about the affairs of this world—how she can please her husband. I am saying this for your own good, not to restrict you, but that you may live in a right way in undivided devotion to the Lord. (1 Cor 7:32-35)[38]

Lastly, we need to recognize what 'time' we are currently in. I know a PhD candidate who is in the last year of his work. He is frustrated with how much time is going into this work when perhaps he could be giving more to the gospel. This discomfort is admirable but given the 'time' he is in, already

---

**38** We will return to the issue of singleness in more depth in chapter 6.

 THE GOOD LIFE IN THE LAST DAYS

so far through the PhD, it makes little sense to stop short of completing and submitting his thesis. But then I know of a medical student who chose to stop their studies early because they intended to go into Christian ministry. They sensed that if they continued on there would be more and more pressure to continue with medical training and work, so they wanted to make a decisive break.

Such observations can wrongly lead some down a path of extreme caution, overly concerned to protect their frailty and anxious to rightly respond to 'where' they are and 'when' they are. In fact, such caution can be a different kind of failure to truly know 'who' you are: a failure to stretch our muscles or exercise our brains leads to atrophy. While being limited, we are also able, to varying degrees, to stretch and struggle and strive. As we look at where we are, we will see many opportunities to say 'Yes' to serving others: from family and friends to church and the wider world. If we close ourselves off from getting 'too involved' in the lives of others at church we might soon find ourselves on the fringes of the community. In particular seasons, even extended seasons, it is good and right to work really hard in ways that might be 'unbalanced' if considered in abstract. Think of the hard work during a summer mission or a church conference. Or think of the devastatingly exhausting but unavoidable and extremely important duties of caring for a newborn baby or a dying relative. It would be completely bizarre to insist on a generic work-life balance in such times. As Kevin DeYoung says at the end of *Crazy Busy*:

> I don't want you think that the best thing we can do
> for ourselves and for the world is to take a pass on

every difficult request, live for leisure, and throw ourselves a giant "me party". I don't want you to think that hard work is the problem, or that sacrificing for others is the problem, or that suffering is necessarily the problem. If you have creativity, ambition, and love, you will be busy. We are supposed to disciple the nations. We are supposed to work with our hands. We are supposed to love God with our minds. We are supposed to have babies and take care of them. It's not a sin to be busy. It's not wrong to be active…

It's possible to live your days in a flurry of hard work, serving and bearing burdens, and to do so with the right character and right dependence on God so that it doesn't feel crazy busy.[39]

We should love people as who they are, where they are, when they are; while knowing who we are, where we are and when we are. When you put things in their right place it will be clearer how to love people and use things. Many of the apparent conflicts and contradictions of competing priorities begin to dissolve when we put things in their right place, as a unified whole of a life lived in worship to God.

## Multiple possible decisions: Christian freedom

I don't want to over-promise here; not every conflict and quandary dissolves. There are certainly plenty of seemingly legitimate options: some perhaps better or worse (gospel

---

**39** Kevin DeYoung, *Crazy Busy: A (Mercifully) Short Book about a (Really) Big Problem,* Crossway, Wheaton IL, 2013, p. 102.

preacher vs. sweet biscuit manufacturer), and others not necessarily worse, just different (neurosurgeon vs. medical research scientist). And there are plenty of tangles in this disordered world where we are left choosing between multiple undesirable options. All of this requires us to understand the nature of Christian freedom.

We will come back to this theme in chapter 8, but in brief, we need to realize that there is no single right way for human beings to respond to all the diversity in the world. More, there is not even one single right way for you to respond to *your* particular place in the world and the diversity of priorities you face day to day. Even within the realm of a godly, wise and zealous Christian lifestyle, there are multiple possible paths. There is a liberty the individual Christian enjoys and a responsibility the individual Christian bears to make decisions about their life. Sometimes we might want a prophecy or a church edict or a mentor or a blog post to tell us exactly what to do and yet this is often because we want to avoid the responsibility of making the decision ourselves, wisely but confidently in Christ as we ought. In thinking about the 'shoulds' and 'should nots' of the Christian life we must work hard to preserve Christian liberty.

In practice none of this is simple, especially so because we are perverted by sin and the world is frustrated by the curse. We won't see things clearly and we don't always respond to each other as we ought. Even our well-intentioned efforts will be frustrated apparently by chance. None of this will be easy and none of it is guaranteed to be 'successful' by the measures of this world alone. Nevertheless, this ongoing work of spiritual and moral reflection is our responsibility and privilege.

## Love in the light of the end of the world

Up to this point salvation history has been in the background. We haven't really touched on the fact that in Christ the kingdom of heaven has dawned, that these are now the last days and we eagerly await the return of Christ and the new creation. If we are to love people as who they are, where they are, when they are, then the 'when' of salvation history certainly changes things significantly. As Don Carson writes:

> Inevitably, that means we live with certain tensions. But such tensions are the very stuff of New Testament ethics, precisely because they are the very stuff of New Testament eschatology.[40]

What do these tensions look like in our lives? Does the urgency of the end of the world necessarily overrule other lesser concerns for comfort, health, family, life? Is this not a call to burnout? How are we live at the end of the world?

40  DA Carson, *Love in Hard Places,* Paternoster, Carlisle, 2002, p. 40.

**3**

# A THEOLOGY OF SACRIFICE: SOME DEAD ENDS

Ladies and gentlemen… the Universe as we know it has now been in existence for over one hundred and seventy thousand million billion years and will be ending in a little over half an hour. So, welcome one and all to Milliways, the Restaurant at the End of the Universe![41]

So says Max Quordlepleen to the diners in the second book in Douglas Adams's *Hitchhiker's Guide to the Galaxy* science-fiction comedy series. We Christians know that we are at the end of the universe: Jesus Christ has died for the salvation of his people, has risen from the dead, now rules in heaven and will soon return in judgement and to make all things new. We are in the final phase of God's purposes for this world, the last days (Heb 1:1-2). How do we live in the

---

[41]  Douglas Adams, *The Restaurant at the End of the Universe,* Pan, London, 1980, pp. 90-1.

light of that? Of course, we are not like Douglas Adams' diners at Milliways sitting and enjoying our delicious meals as we wait for the spectacle. Our Lord does not reveal to us his timetable simply so we can make our way in an orderly fashion to the designated departure points, as if our only duty were to withdraw and wait. These last days are the gospel age where his will is that the good news be preached to all nations before he returns (Matt 24:14; Acts 1:7-8; 2 Pet 3:8-9). This changes our whole approach to life so that what would otherwise be normal and good becomes inappropriate:

> From now on those who have wives should live as if they do not; those who mourn, as if they did not; those who are happy, as if they were not; those who buy something, as if it were not theirs to keep; those who use the things of the world, as if not engrossed in them. For this world in its present form is passing away. (1 Cor 7:29-31)

But what exactly does this look like? What does it mean to 'live as if' you were not married or 'live as if' you were not happy? To 'live as if' your purchases were not yours to keep or 'live as if' not engrossed in the things that we use every day? What does this lifestyle look like in practical terms? How should it affect our decisions? In this chapter we will consider some dead ends and inadequate answers and then I will go on to unpack a more satisfactory and comprehensive biblical answer.

## Crisis ethics: everything is up for grabs because Jesus is coming back tomorrow

One approach to the shock of texts like 1 Corinthians 7 is to read them as if written by people who thought Jesus was coming back in a matter of weeks, months or years, rather than decades, centuries or millennia. In this context, so the argument goes, new rules apply. Such an imminent return, they say, brings with it "the end of all civilisation and its values"[42] and so "demands mighty acts, sometimes super-human acts… things that would be simply impossible under ordinary circumstances".[43] This view involves speculation about how Jesus and his apostles thought about the end of the world: that because they said things like "the time is short" and "the night is nearly over" and Jesus is "coming soon" they expected this to be very, very soon. And given Christ did not in fact return straight away, this view has a low view of Scripture, seeing it as a flawed document written by mistaken authors. Actually it is the theologians who are mistaken! They misread the meaning of these time statements. As Anthony Thiselton explains, they confuse a "theological stance" of immanence [this is the last phase of God's purposes, God will complete his purposes next] with a "chronological estimate" of immanence [Jesus is literally coming back next week]."[44] The time we now live in is the time where there is nothing that stands between us and the events surrounding the return of Christ, our whole outlook

42 Wolfgang Schrage summarizing Schweitzer in *The Ethics of the New Testament,* trans. DE Green, T&T Clark, Edinburgh, 1988, p. 31.
43 Weiss cited in Schrage, *The Ethics of the New Testament,* p. 30.
44 Antony C Thiselton, *Paul's First Letter to the Corinthians,* Eerdmans, Grand Rapids, MI, 2000, p. 578.

and orientation is waiting for the return of Christ, whether he comes in days or millennia, as Peter writes:

> But do not forget this one thing, dear friends: With the Lord a day is like a thousand years, and a thousand years are like a day. The Lord is not slow in keeping his promise, as some understand slowness. Instead he is patient with you, not wanting anyone to perish, but everyone to come to repentance.
>
> But the day of the Lord will come like a thief. (2 Pet 3:8-10a)

Even if we knew Jesus were actually to return in a matter of months, I am not convinced that this calls for moral chaos. Should I not care for my family if Christ is coming back in a few days? Am I free to steal from you since Jesus will come in glory in the spring? Although priorities might shift depending on the times we are in, the underlying realities of good and evil, right and wrong don't change. The chilling novel *On the Beach* by Nevil Shute provides a very plausible portrayal of this kind of thing. In the novel, the Southern Hemisphere awaits the inevitable and deadly arrival of lethal radiation from a massive nuclear conflict. At first Melbourne society descends into chaos and sensuality. But with time, many return to more regular patterns of life: planting gardens, learning to touch type and engaging in military duties. No matter what the timeline, the good things of life remain good.[45]

I think this is the meaning of the famous saying, that people claim was said by Martin Luther (but probably

---

45  Nevil Shute, *On the Beach,* Vintage Classics, London, 2009.

wasn't): "Even if I knew that tomorrow the world would go to pieces, I would plant an apple tree today".[46] Stanley Hauerwas points out that this is what separates us from the doomsday cults, who lose connection with the reality and goodness of this creation and so can justify mass suicides like at Jonestown.[47]

## Stoic philosophy: Don't get entangled with unimportant worldly things

Others point out that the biblical passages about self-denial have a lot in common with the teachings of Stoic philosophers, who saw all comforts of the world, even life itself, as having little value. Perhaps the real reason for the apostle Paul commending singleness, for example, is because he

46  Another variation of this approach, in the case of 1 Corinthians 7, is that there was a particular famine 'crisis' at the time of writing, that called for an emergency lifestyle, as an extra motivation in addition to the reality of the last days (Bruce Winter, *After Paul Left Corinth: The Influence of Secular Ethics and Social Change,* Eerdmans, Grand Rapids, MI, 2001, pp. 216-24, 241-52). I'm not persuaded that this is needed to understand 1 Corinthians 7. The reasoning of 1 Corinthians 7 is much more general than that. Paul speaks of the overall merit of singleness as opposed to marriage in verses 32-35, which doesn't really depend on famine to be true. Also, clearly one of the reasons for his instruction is that "this world in its present form is passing away", so it is unnecessary, unless there are very strong reasons, to imagine an additional 'crisis' is in view. Besides, the instruction doesn't really make sense of a famine crisis: why would a temporary famine be a good reason not to make a lifelong decision about marriage? Marriage can bring together strong bonds of care and support that would be very beneficial in a time of famine, surely? And famines don't last forever, do they?

47  Stanley Hauerwas, 'Sex in Public: How Adventurous Christians are Doing It (1978)', in John Berkman and Michael Cartwright (eds), *The Hauerwas Reader,* Duke University Press, Durham, 2001, p. 498. See also Hauerwas, 'On Taking Religion Seriously: The Challenge of Jonestown (1982)' in *Against the Nations: War and Survival in a Liberal Society,* Winston Press, Minneapolis, 1985.

values high, spiritual matters more than low, worldly matters. The Stoic philosopher Epictetus questioned whether it would not be better for a man "to be free from distraction, wholly devoted to the service of God" rather than "tied down by the private duties of men… For see, he must show certain service to his father-in-law, to the rest of his wife's relatives, to his wife herself; finally, he is driven from his profession, to act as a nurse in his own family and to provide for them."[48] Compare this with what Paul says in 1 Corinthians 7:32-35:

> I would like you to be free from concern. An unmarried man is concerned about the Lord's affairs—how he can please the Lord. But a married man is concerned about the affairs of this world—how he can please his wife—and his interests are divided. An unmarried woman or virgin is concerned about the Lord's affairs: Her aim is to be devoted to the Lord in both body and spirit. But a married woman is concerned about the affairs of this world—how she can please her husband. I am saying this for your own good, not to restrict you, but that you may live in a right way in undivided devotion to the Lord.

There is a surface similarity, and a genuine truth both agree on: a single life enables a person to be more single-minded. There is a depth and intensity and quantity of good that can be done by a person who is not divided by other competing concerns. A single person might be able to give themselves

48 *Epictetus,* Discourses, Loeb Classic Library, Harvard University Press, book III, p. 155 (viewed 19 October 2017): www.loebclassics.com/view/epictetus-discourses/1925/pb_LCL218.155.xml?readMode=recto

 THE GOOD LIFE IN THE LAST DAYS

with particular intensity to research, or exploration, or prayer and Bible study, or charitable work and frontier missions because they are not absorbed with marriage and child rearing. On this point, Christians and Stoics can agree. Perhaps we could even do the thought experiment: if Adam and Eve never rebelled would there have been some human beings who would have lived a single life, given to exploration, study, prayer—who can say? A single life is not an inadequate or incomplete life. In fact, the single life has unique benefits.[49]

But while there is a truth in the Stoic perspective, there are also big differences between it and the perspective of the Bible. *The Bible gives us a much higher view of worldly things.* Remember chapter 1? God made things other than himself. We worship and serve him in and through everything we do. It is good and right and holy and spiritual to marry, make love and raise children. It is good and right and holy to buy and sell things, to build and plant things.

When God describes the single man or woman as "concerned about the Lord's affairs… in undivided devotion to the Lord" he is not denying that a married Christian serves the Lord in their marriage. This is their God-given duty according to verse 3 and it is their calling according to verse 17. He is speaking comparatively rather than absolutely. When compared to the diverse ways in which the married Christian serves the Lord, the single Christian has the opportunity to focus on a narrower group of activities that are more directly concerned with God's word and work. Of course we serve the Lord in every area of our lives, but

49 We will return to the issue of singleness in more depth in chapter 6.

when we are engaged with the Bible and prayer we are more explicitly and directly engaging with "the work of the Lord" (see 1 Cor 15:58 and 16:10). Comparatively speaking, the word and prayer are more important things than what he calls "the affairs of this world" in verses 33-34. We can and should think and speak in this kind of comparative way, without undermining the broader truths we explored in chapter 1.[50]

Furthermore, *the dominant reason Paul gives for the sacrificial life in verses 29-31 is not that marriage, or emotions or property are of low value, but the particular time we are in:* "What I mean, brothers and sisters, is that the time is short… For this world in its present form is passing away." He is commending a 'living as if' stance towards things that are in and of themselves good things but which should be held lightly because of the time we are in. This is even clearer when we think about the ultimate Christian hope, of a new creation enjoyed in resurrected bodies. Our 'living as if' is only a temporary stance as we wait for eternity. As Charles Taylor explains:

> The Stoic sage is willing to give up… health, freedom, or life, because he sees it genuinely as without value… The Christian martyr, in giving up health, freedom, or life, doesn't declare them to be of no value. On the

50 In chapter 5 of *The Things of Earth,* Joe Rigney categorizes two ways that the Bible speaks about our attitude to the things of this world: 1) The Comparative Approach reminds us that God is infinitely more valuable than anything else in his creation. 2) The Integrative Approach shows us how we honour and worship God in and through everything we do, including enjoying the things of this world. He says that we live out the Integrative Approach each day, while using the Comparative Approach as a regular test and reminder to order everything rightly.

     THE GOOD LIFE IN THE LAST DAYS

contrary, the action would lose its sense if they were not of great worth.[51]

The call to self-denial cannot be explained by some kind of crisis ethic because Jesus is coming back really soon. Nor can it be explained by a fundamental lack of value in physical and worldly things. How else can we approach these challenging commands? I now want to turn from more academic and theoretical explanations to some more 'commonsense' approaches: 'sensible sacrifice', 'sensing sacrifice' and 'similar sacrifices'.

## Sensible sacrifice: Work-life balance, even in extraordinary circumstances

The first 'commonsense solution' affirms that the time we live in means we should live with an urgency and self-sacrifice… but not be too extreme about it. There are a lot of Christian books and seminars out there which bring this perspective.[52] They rightly remind us of our human limits: our need for rest and the importance of investing in key relationships. Even in emergency situations there is only so long that medical teams and rescue teams can go without rest before their whole emergency effort collapses. To be useful for the kingdom of God, for those we love and for the needy of the world, we need to look after our mental, physical and spiritual health. Otherwise we'll end up

**51**  Taylor, *Sources of the Self,* p. 218.
**52**  See for example *Zeal Without Burnout* by Christopher Ash and *Going the Distance: How to Stay Fit for a Lifetime of Ministry* by Peter Brain (Matthias Media, Sydney, 2004).

needing to be ministered to by someone else, rather than continuing in our ministry. We are no good to the relief effort if we become incapacitated. In fact, we become a drain on resources.

This insight is terrific, so far as it goes. But it is lacking for two reasons. *Firstly, this kind of approach is theologically thin.* Books and seminars on this topic normally don't set out to be theologically rich, so there's nothing wrong with them in and of themselves. However, it becomes a problem if all Christians ever get in this area is a reminder of our creaturely limitation, the importance of the Sabbath and a reminder that Jesus himself withdrew to rest sometimes. We still need help integrating these truths with everything else the Bible teaches. How does this relate to our understanding of the last days, our view of sin, or the priority of the gospel mission? This lack of theological depth can lead to earnest Christians taking a day off because they know it's sensible, but still feeling an underlying sense of guilt that they are not *really* living in the light of the return of Christ.

*A second problem with this approach is that it runs the risk of drifting into the kind of overly cautious self-concern I mentioned in the Introduction.* Those who have suffered from burnout can sometimes become understandably reactionary to any exhortation to hard work and self-sacrifice out of fear that it will lead to the kind of awful pain they have experienced in the past. While understandable, this is not the best outlook for God's people as a whole. As Christopher Ash's little book is rightly titled, we want "*zeal* without burnout".

For this reason, ministry common sense often supplements this 'work-life balance' approach of sensible sacrifice with the second commonsense approach: sensing sacrifice.

　　　　　THE GOOD LIFE IN THE LAST DAYS

## Sensing sacrifice: If it hurts a bit you're probably doing it right

This simple test asks us if we are serving God with such reserve that we don't feel any discomfort at all. Is such service appropriate? Surely a good indication we are living Christianly is that we feel some degree of discomfort? Something of this instinct comes out in Francis Chan and Danae Yankoski's *Crazy Love*. As they describe the 'lukewarm Christian' the criticism seems in part to be on their failure to meet a standard of 'crazy love'. These 'lukewarm Christians':

> …give money to charity and to the church… as long as it doesn't impinge on their standard of living. If they have a little extra and it is easy and safe to give, they do so. After all, God loves a cheerful giver, right?

> …are moved by stories about people who do radical things for Christ, yet they do not act. They assume such action is for 'extreme' Christians, not average ones. Lukewarm people call 'radical' what Jesus expected of all his followers.

> …gauge their morality or 'goodness' by comparing themselves to the secular world. They feel satisfied that while they aren't as hard-core for Jesus as so-and-so, they are nowhere as horrible as the guy down the street.

> …love God, but they do not love Him with all their heart, soul, and strength. They would be quick to assure you that they try to love God that much, but that sort of devotion isn't really possible for the average person; it's only for pastors and missionaries and radicals.

…will serve God and others, but there are limits to how far they will go or how much time, money, and energy they are willing to give.

…think about life on earth much more often than eternity in heaven. Daily life is mostly focused on today's to-do list, this week's schedule, and next month's vacation. Rarely, if ever, do they intently consider the life to come.[53]

As with 'sensible sacrifice', this works well as a common-sense rule of thumb. If our approach to life is to always do things easily within our capacity we are hardly using our full potential, whether in study, sport or serving others. It is right to stretch ourselves and make every effort in doing good. How much more should we work hard for the cause of the gospel in these last days! In this way 'sensing' sacrifice is a simple way to help us keep striving. Have I grown comfortable in my contribution to the kingdom of God? Or am I seeking first his kingdom and his righteousness? Am I loving the Lord with all my heart and mind and soul and strength?

It's a helpful test but an inadequate one. Sensing sacrifice doesn't cope well with the fact that often we can find great pleasure in doing what is good, even at great cost to ourselves. The more we delight in the Lord and genuinely desire the good of others, the more we find ourselves delighting in doing what will honour God and serve others, even if it is to our detriment, on a superficial level. Paul describes this in reference to both parenting and Christian leadership in 2 Corinthians 12:14-15: "After all, children should not have

---

53 Francis Chan with Danae Yankoski, *Crazy Love: Overwhelmed by a Relentless God*, David C Cook, Ontario, 2013, pp. 68-80.

to save up for their parents, but parents for their children. So I will very gladly spend for you everything I have and expend myself as well." I have just come from the Geneva Push church planting conference where I heard someone speak about when she first raised the bar of commitment for Sunday School teachers in her church. Instead of being rostered on for only a few days a month she began to ask them commit to teach Sunday School weekly for a whole term. But as she asked more from them (with all the work and inconvenience this entailed) they began to build deeper relationships with the kids they were teaching, and see them making progress in learning, and so take more pleasure and satisfaction in the ministry. In the end, the Term 1 teachers asked if they could be rostered on again for Term 3![54]

This 'if it hurts' test is also clumsy, because the significance of an action is not in direct proportion to its negative effects on us. Sometimes, the best thing to do happens to also be the easiest! Sometimes, 'radical' living makes a negligible difference in the big scheme of things. At worst, it can generate the absurd approach to life that as long as everything is just a bit uncomfortable and everyone is just slightly miserable, then we are honouring the Lord. We can even begin to value unpleasantness for its own sake, regardless of its tangible benefit for anyone or anything. A mother can work herself half to death in a kind of martyrdom that her children don't need or want, more out of her own need to be needed. A

---

54 Joe Rigney in *The Things of Earth* says, "There is a way of embracing sacrifice and hardship and inconvenience (however great or small) that will be identified by some as a kind of enjoyment. You will look like you are having too much of a good time. You will spend yourself and be spent, and you will do so with a twinkle in your eye and laughter in your heart" (p. 183).

workaholic can hang back at the office doing needless busy work and jump at the ringing of their phone for enquiries that can wait, ultimately because they have become addicted to the buzz of adrenaline.

We must make sure that in pursuing biblical self-denial we do not slide into the pagan error of asceticism (like the Stoics, above), that sees merit in renouncing the physical world for its own sake:

> Since you died with Christ to the elemental spiritual forces of this world, why, as though you still belonged to the world, do you submit to its rules: "Do not handle! Do not taste! Do not touch!"? These rules, which have to do with things that are all destined to perish with use, are based on merely human commands and teachings. Such regulations indeed have an appearance of wisdom, with their self-imposed worship, their false humility and their harsh treatment of the body, but they lack any value in restraining sensual indulgence. (Col 2:20-23)

As Christians, who believe in a good creation and a physical resurrection, our attitude to life in this world is positive, but reserved: we seek to glorify God by receiving his good gifts with thanksgiving, while being alert to the ways in which sin so easily distorts our attitudes. We need a richer approach than this, something like what GK Chesterton is reaching for in this lovely passage:

> We do not want joy and anger to neutralize each other and produce a surly contentment; we want a fiercer delight and a fiercer discontent. We have to feel the

    THE GOOD LIFE IN THE LAST DAYS

universe at once as an ogre's castle, to be stormed, and yet as our own cottage, to which we can return at evening.[55]

## Similar sacrifices: working off thought experiments and analogies

The gospel is like the cure to a virus that is killing the entire human race; it is like a lifeboat for all those billions drowning in a great sea of judgement, like the one way out of a burning building. What would *you* do if you had a miracle cure? We use such thought experiments to stir each other to urgent evangelistic action. But they are very limited in their usefulness. Let's leave aside the hardening effect of sin and the need for a supernatural work of the Holy Spirit to illuminate the hard heart of the unbeliever and consider the thought experiment on its own terms. Would door-knocking and friendship evangelism and public information events be the way to bring a miracle cure to billions of human beings? We would need pharmaceutical testing, safe production and efficient channels of distribution. The process would require detailed reports and high-level international meetings to ensure effective collaboration. Perhaps there would even be the kinds of individual, social and political blockages caused by all sorts of pettiness, ignorance, human error and corruption. Soon this urgent miracle cure scenario starts to look a lot like the church today! While the thought experiment is a vivid challenge, which might help us keep things in perspective, it doesn't easily map out next steps for the

55　GK Chesterton, *Orthodoxy,* John Lane Company, 1908, p. 4.

individual believer or local church.

John Piper has used another analogy: wartime. He writes:

In wartime, the newspapers carry headlines about how the troops are doing. In wartime, families talk about the sons and daughters on the front lines and write to them and pray for them with heart-wrenching concern for their safety. In wartime, we are on alert. We are armed. We are vigilant. In wartime, we spend money differently—there is austerity, not for its own sake but because there are more strategic ways to spend money than on new tires at home. The war effort touches everybody. We all cut back. The luxury liner becomes a troop carrier.[56]

This analogy is more in line with explicit scriptural teaching, as it picks up on 2 Timothy 2:3-4. "Join with me in suffering, like a good soldier of Christ Jesus. No-one serving as a soldier gets entangled in civilian affairs, but rather tries to please his commanding officer." Except in Piper's analogy we are not all soldiers. Rather many of us are on "the home front". That is because Piper's analogy is not drawn from first-century military service, but the unique experience of the two World Wars of the 20th century. In applying this analogy, care has to be taken not to make experience of wartime austerity in 1941 the gold standard of the Christian life, in a kind of severe sentimentality. Young idealistic Christian men (like I used to be), captivated by the ideal of macho 'wartime gospel lifestyle' use it to justify the kind of

**56** John Piper, *Let the Nations Be Glad,* 3rd edn, Baker, Grand Rapids, MI, 2010, p. 65. Cited in Rigney, *The Things of Earth,* p. 198.

 THE GOOD LIFE IN THE LAST DAYS

Spartan approach to life that appeals to idealistic young men anyway, and then smugly look down on others.[57] Such young idealists can sometimes despise the "home front" not appreciating that it is their mothers, wives or friends who are washing their clothes, cooking their food and paying their way.[58] Our mental picture needs to be padded out with the realism and humanity of real armies made up of regular people. Kevin DeYoung and Greg Gilbert point out, "We may be at war, but even soldiers get ice cream sometimes,"[59] and CS Lewis, speaking from personal experience:

> Before I went to the last war I certainly expected that my life in the trenches would, in some mysterious sense, be all war. In fact, I found that the nearer you got to the front line the less everyone spoke and thought of the allied cause and the progress of the campaign… Christians and soldiers are still men: the

---

**57** "But here's the thing. None of that was very hard. I didn't want to wear expensive clothes. I liked my roommates. And I think ramen noodles are actually pretty tasty. So living the wartime lifestyle wasn't really a sacrifice. Although the wartime metaphor did add biblical warrant to lifestyle choices I had already made, giving them a holy veneer and texture, my satisfaction in my strategic lifestyle was far out of proportion to the degree of sacrifice. Giving up things that you don't want anyway is easy, and it's a minefield of pride and smugness." (Rigney, *The Things of Earth*, p. 203.)

**58** At what point does such frugal sacrifice become the kind of stinginess that Proverbs warns of?

"Do not eat the food of a begrudging host,
    do not crave his delicacies;
for he is the kind of person
    who is always thinking about the cost.
'Eat and drink,' he says to you,
    but his heart is not with you.
You will vomit up the little you have eaten
    and will have wasted your compliments." (Prov 23:6-8)

**59** DeYoung and Gilbert, *Mission of the Church,* p. 264.

infidel's idea of the religious life, and the civilian's idea of active service, are [a fantasy].[60]

A simpler thought experiment simply asks 'What would Jesus do?' or 'What would the apostle Paul do?' Can you imagine Jesus staying home from work with a cold? Can you imagine the apostle Paul going to Fiji on Long Service Leave? If not, how can we justify it? Of course this train of thought is built on an argument from silence, with the building materials of our imagination. We don't really know the details of Jesus or Paul's rhythms of work and rest and recreation, at least not in detail. So we are left imagining what it might be like. The thought experiment does not advance our thinking very far, because it really requires us to draw on our pre-existing assumptions about what is right. Indeed some little fragments we do have suggest a fuller picture: Jesus came eating and drinking, so that he was called a glutton and a drunkard (Matt 11:19), and he also withdrew to quiet places from time to time (Matt 14:13); Paul learned the secret of being content while well fed and living in plenty (Phil 4:11-12) and taught that God gives us good things to enjoy (1 Tim 6:17). But I don't want to go too far down this line, of trying to pull together bits and pieces of a portrait to then fuel our attempts to reconstruct what Jesus or Paul would think about going to see a musical or eating Yum Cha.

Rather than thinking about miracle cures to global

60  CS Lewis, 'Learning in War-Time', 1939. Lewis preached this sermon to students at Oxford, answering the question 'How can you justify academic pursuits during World War II?' Accessed from *Bradley G Green*, 22 August 2011 (viewed 25 October 2017): www.bradleyggreen.com/attachments/Lewis.Learning%20in%20War-Time.pdf

                    THE GOOD LIFE IN THE LAST DAYS

viruses, wartime austerity and apostolic holidays, a better way forward is to let God's word teach us the right way to live. We should listen to the teaching of Jesus and Paul, rather than try to imagine what they would do. What practical teaching do we find in Scripture about how to live in the last days?

*Firstly, we are to live godly lives.* The reality of the imminent return of Christ is a motivation to "keep watch" and "be ready" as Jesus' parables teach in Matthew 24-25. If we live godless lives, then when he returns, we will be surprised and left behind. 2 Peter 3 is a great example of this:

> Since everything will be destroyed in this way, what kind of people ought you to be? You ought to live holy and godly lives as you look forward to the day of God and speed its coming.[61] That day will bring about the destruction of the heavens by fire, and the elements will melt in the heat. But in keeping with his promise we are looking forward to a new heaven and a new earth, where righteousness dwells.
>
> So then, dear friends, since you are looking forward to this, make every effort to be found spotless, blameless and at peace with him. (vv. 11-14)

Likewise Romans 13:

> And do this, understanding the present time: the hour has already come for you to wake up from your slumber, because our salvation is nearer now than when we

---

61   It is hard to see how we might 'speed' the coming of the Lord, since he will return at the time determined by his Father. Better to go with the NIV footnote 'wait eagerly' (so also the Holman Christian Standard Bible).

first believed. The night is nearly over; the day is almost here. So let us put aside the deeds of darkness and put on the armour of light. Let us behave decently, as in the daytime, not in carousing and drunkenness, not in sexual immorality and debauchery, not in dissension and jealousy. Rather, clothe yourselves with the Lord Jesus Christ, and do not think about how to gratify the desires of the flesh. (vv. 11-14)

*Secondly, we are urged to invest in eternal things.* Jesus' end-time parables in Matthew 24-25 teach that as his servants wait for him to return we ought to care for his household and invest his riches. In 2 Timothy, Paul's solemn charge to Timothy is framed by the second coming, and it urges him to focus on the preaching the word:

In the presence of God and of Christ Jesus, who will judge the living and the dead, and in view of his appearing and his kingdom, I give you this charge: Preach the word; be prepared in season and out of season; correct, rebuke and encourage—with great patience and careful instruction… keep your head in all situations, endure hardship, do the work of an evangelist, discharge all the duties of your ministry. (2 Tim 4:1-2, 5)

Interestingly, words like 'urgently', 'quickly' and 'hurry' are not often used in the New Testament. We are told in Acts 6:7 that the number of disciples increased rapidly, and the Thessalonians are urged to pray that the message of the Lord may spread rapidly (2 Thess 3:1)—we would *like* the gospel to spread quickly. But 'urgent' or 'hurried' might not be the best words to describe the character of the Christian life. I suggest 'strong concern and focussed attention on eternal things' is a better way to put it. That is why the wartime analogy is the most appropriate. But whether or not we choose to use analogies and thought experiments, we need spiritual wisdom shaped by God's word to discern the most appropriate way to apply these principles, given who we are and where we find ourselves.

## The way forward: must be objective and must be subjective

So is there a better way? Can we hold together living well with living rightly? Can we pursue zeal without promoting burnout? Can we die to self while delighting in the Lord?

*The way forward must be objective*: it must recognize that this world is a real world. More than that: it is our heavenly Father's good-but-fallen-creation. He made it, and to live according to his word is the way to live well in it. The last days and the second coming don't erase the world but look forward to its renewal. Oliver O'Donovan warns us against a kingdom ethic becoming just a "Zen riddle". There is a danger of talking about the tension of living in the last days in such a way that the new creation loses its "comprehensibility, hence its worldliness… and becomes merely a transcendent mystery."[62] My goal is to take us beyond commonsense slogans and rules of thumb about 'balance' and 'wisdom' and 'feeling it' to a whole vision for living well as Christians in God's good-but-fallen-creation in these last days.

*The way forward must also be subjectively relevant.* It must

---

62  O'Donovan, *Resurrection and Moral Order,* pp. 143-5.

actually apply to the real and wonderful mix of diverse people Christ has bought with his own blood. And it must apply to all the varied circumstances we find ourselves in. Absolute rules and ideals are not enough if they don't actually map well onto real lives in real homes. Because as we saw in chapter 1: the different expressions of the Christian life aren't a problem that needs fixing, but are part of the glorious diversity that our heavenly Father has brought forth.

*The way forward must be good and be felt to be good.* If sacrificing ourselves for the cause of the gospel is actually how to live well in these last days, then it is the best way to live, and it is possible to actually perceive and experience it as good. Not only will it be possible but it will be somehow wonderful. Not that it will be simple or easy or comfortable; but it will be wonderful in a deep and rich way that surpasses even rational comprehension and emotional stability.

**4**

# A THEOLOGY OF SACRIFICE: A CATALOGUE OF SACRIFICE AND SUFFERING

In our evangelism it is important to talk about both the Christian gospel and the Christian life. Ordinarily we don't just present the gospel, and hold off on discussions of ethics until a person has put their faith in Christ. One obvious reason for this is that we cannot understand why Jesus died unless we understand the nature of sin, and we cannot understand the nature of sin unless we understand the original good order of creation. A vision of the goodness of human beings ruling God's world under his loving rule sets us up to see the ugly and pathetic nature of sin and the great need for Jesus' rescue.[63] Another reason we need to talk about the Christian life in our evangelism is that we are seeking to make disciples, not merely decisions. A simplistic

---

63  This is a reason the *Two Ways to Live* gospel outline is so helpful in evangelism. See www.matthiasmedia.com.au/2wtl/ for more information.

gospel invitation can backfire, especially in a context where people are biblically illiterate. People think they are responding to an easy offer of divine blessing for their life, and fail to grasp the purpose and goal of salvation. Repentance always accompanies true faith, and joyful obedience is the genuine and inevitable outworking of salvation by grace alone. A final reason we need to talk about the Christian life in our evangelism is that it answers an objection many people have: what's the fine print of the mobile phone contract called 'Christianity'? Saved by grace through faith sounds great… but what do I have to do? What do I have to give up? Do I need to start liking board games and Christian soft rock music and scrapbooking? Will I live a hard, painful, miserable life?

How would you describe the Christian life in an evangelistic conversation? On the one hand, we could speak of it in beautiful and positive terms: in Christ we truly flourish as human beings. We have every spiritual blessing in him: election, holiness, predestination, adoption, redemption, forgiveness, knowledge of the mysteries of God's will, the seal of the Holy Spirit, the hope to which he has called us, his great power for us who believe (Eph 1:3-19). The Christian life is not a small, sad, suffocating thing. It truly is 'the good life'.

But on the other hand, we need to also speak about counting the cost. As Jesus warns:

> "Suppose one of you wants to build a tower. Won't you first sit down and estimate the cost to see if you have enough money to complete it? For if you lay the foundation and are not able to finish it, everyone who

          THE GOOD LIFE IN THE LAST DAYS

sees it will ridicule you, saying, 'This person began to build and wasn't able to finish'.

Or suppose a king is about to go to war against another king. Won't he first sit down and consider whether he is able with ten thousand men to oppose the one coming against him with twenty thousand? If he is not able, he will send a delegation while the other is still a long way off and will ask for terms of peace. In the same way, those of you who do not give up everything you have cannot be my disciples." (Luke 14:28-33)

Such tough talk is crucial to warn off the insincere, shallow, selfish disciple. Such a warning makes sure that they begin the Christian life on the right foundation.

But how do these two true perspectives fit together? Is it enriching to be a Christian? Or costly? Do Christians experience blessing? Or suffering? Is it all physical and emotional suffering in this world, with spiritual blessing now, and physical blessing only when Christ returns? Not quite. An important thing is to realize that only some of the sacrifices in the Christian life are really sacrifices of something good. Some so-called sacrifices are only sacrifices in a more qualified, relative sense. In this chapter we are going to catalogue different kinds of suffering and sacrifice as follows:

- Sacrificing one good thing for another
- Dying to our sinful selves
- Suffering in a fallen world
- Suffering for the sake of Christ
- Treating this world as temporary and knowing the time is short

And in the chapter that follows we will explore how even the costliness of following Christ is the best way to live life in God's good-but-fallen-creation in these last days.

## Sacrificing one good thing for another

One of the great films of 2016 was *La La Land,* a joyful, colourful old-school musical. While having all the bells and whistles on a superficial level, it has emotional depth as well. The final sequence (no spoilers!) is powerful because it gives us a bittersweet picture of an alternative history of *what could have been.* It is sweet because the actual reality is a happy ending as it is; it is bitter because the alternate reality would have also been a happy ending. That's a particular kind of mourning we all know and experience: the loss that comes with the passing of time and the particularity of life. We mourn childhood as we enter puberty, we grieve the loss of friends who move overseas for great job opportunities, we daydream wistfully about how our lives might have turned out differently. But none of this is bad. None of this is a result of the curse that has come upon our world because of the judgement of God. In some way there will be elements of these 'losses' in the new creation too. Because they are the inevitable result of the limited, finite nature of the created world: we are not God, we have limits, we can't do everything and be everywhere at once.

Some of the 'sacrifices' we make for the sake of following Christ are really in this category. That is, they are not ultimately accepting evil experiences, they are just going a different way. Giving up an enjoyable and challenging and high-paying career in order to preach the gospel full-time is sacrificing one good thing for another, as is missing out on the joys of family life for the freedom of singleness, as is budgeting to give up some creature comforts in order to be more generous to a charity. The sense of loss is real, but it is not a curse. When we make these decisions for larger reasons (whether those be goals, moral values or gospel priorities) these driving reasons become a motivator and compensator: we are doing it for some greater good. But it is only 'making sacrifices' or 'denying yourself' in a soft sense.

## Dying to our sinful selves

Another kind of dying to ourselves is, again, only a relative loss: it is dying to our *sinful* selves, so that we might honour God as the rightful Lord over our lives. This is a big part of what Jesus is speaking of in Mark 8 when he says:

> "Whoever wants to be my disciple must deny themselves and take up their cross and follow me. For whoever wants to save their life will lose it, but whoever loses their life for me and for the gospel will save it. What good is it for someone to gain the whole world, yet forfeit their soul? Or what can anyone give in exchange for their soul? If anyone is ashamed of me and my words in this adulterous and sinful generation, the Son of Man will be ashamed of them when he comes in his Father's glory with the holy angels." (vv. 34-39)

There are two concepts woven together in this passage: mention of 'taking up their cross' and 'losing their life' brings with it the concept of martyrdom for the sake of Christ

—more of that below; the concepts of 'denying themselves' and 'gaining the whole world' suggest something different: dying to the sinful self who lives with no regard for God. The old self, enslaved to sin and facing the wrath of God, must die in a "moment of self-annihilation".[64] But this is a good thing, to leave that sinful self behind, to be made new by the grace of God (Eph 4:22-23).

That is the fundamental challenge of Luke 14 as well: "If anyone comes to me and does not hate father and mother, wife and children, brothers and sisters—yes, even their own life—such a person cannot be my disciple" (v. 26). The point of Jesus' powerful rhetoric is not that we must conjure up feelings of hatred for our family members. The point is that our devotion to him must be so strong that by comparison, our devotion to our family could be described, with a bit of linguistic license, as 'hatred'. In the simplest cases where our family, or our own preferences, contradict the command of Christ, then we must literally hate their counsel: we must obey God rather than men. But what if we love art or sport or work or ambition more than Christ? What if we make them our driving concern, allowing their demands to lead us to disobey the commands of Christ? Then we must sacrifice our worldly, sinful love of them. Likewise, if we boast in our ethnic heritage, ritual purity and religious performance, in the hope that such things will draw the blessing of God, we must, as Paul puts it, "consider them garbage, that [we] may gain Christ... not having a righteousness of [our] own... but that which is through faith in Christ" (Phil 3:8b-9a).

64  O'Donovan, *Resurrection and Moral Order,* p. 112.

   THE GOOD LIFE IN THE LAST DAYS

Now such 'sacrifice' is only a relative sacrifice. It's a sacrifice of our sinful selves, of idolatrous devotion, of worldly desire.[65] Such dying is killing things not worth having; it is coming to find true life as it is really meant to be. It can be described as a loss or sacrifice or cost only because that's what it looks like to a sinful human being. But once we trust Christ, die to our sinful selves and follow him, we find that we have found the life that is truly life, and the things we have left behind are not as precious as we thought they were.

Not all suffering is a matter of perception, however. In this fallen, cursed world, there are not only relative sacrifices, but real, evil hardships.

## Suffering in a fallen world

All human beings experience pain and suffering that is the result of God's curse on the world and, as long as Christians continue to live in this age, we are not immune to this kind of suffering. The world is disordered and decaying, we do not experience clarity, justice and peace, but instead confusion, injustice and turmoil. We suffer from natural disasters, terminal illnesses, economic collapse, inter-personal conflict, corruption, oppression, bullying and abuse. Those who do the right thing, whether Christian or not, also suffer

---

**65**  In 1 John 2:15-17, we are commanded not to love "the 'world', or anything in the world". But John defines "the world" as "the lust of the flesh, the lust of the eyes, and the pride of life". Joe Rigney talks about the Bible's Comparative Approach to things of this world, that emphasizes the incomparable worth of God, to warn against a worldly and idolatrous attitude to the things of this world. See footnote 50.

in particular ways, because in a sinful world some people are hostile to righteousness.

This kind of suffering is not unique to being a Christian, and so it is not a sacrifice we make for the sake of following Christ in particular. But there is a uniquely Christian experience of this kind of general suffering, that is a wonderful blessing. Because of God's word, we can understand the reason for the general suffering of the world and consider whether there are any particular reasons for the suffering we are experiencing. Because of God's sanctifying work, we can grow virtues of patience, trust, hope, compassion and humility (Rom 5:3-4). And because of the gospel of Christ, we have hope for the future without suffering, when our Father will "wipe every tear from [our] eyes" and "there will be no more death or mourning or crying or pain" (Rev 21:4). We know that Christ also suffered and so can sympathize with us in our suffering (Heb 4:14-5:10) and that the Holy Spirit is in us and groans within us and helps us when we don't know what to pray for (Rom 8:22-27).[66]

In addition to this, we Christians embrace the difficulties of life as a sacrifice borne for the sake of God's purposes. The only reason God's people suffer is because Christ has not returned yet. And there are only two reasons that Christ has not returned in glory: that he might be glorified as his people are sanctified through suffering, and that the gospel might be preached to the lost. Because we also value the importance of gospel preaching, we Christians are torn between the "desire to depart and be with Christ, which is better by far"

---

66 See for example Tim Keller's superb book *Walking with God through Pain and Suffering,* Hodder & Stoughton, London, 2013.

 THE GOOD LIFE IN THE LAST DAYS

and the desire to "go on living in the body [which] will mean fruitful labour for" the gospel (Phil 1:21-24). We share the mind of God the Father, who is "patient… not wanting anyone to perish, but everyone to come to repentance" (2 Pet 3:9). So we need to learn to faithfully submit to the timing of our heavenly Father, as we suffer in this life and cry "Come, Lord Jesus!" (Rev 22:20)

## Suffering for the sake of Christ

This world is in rebellion against God, and so this world will hate those who love God:

> "Blessed are you when people insult you, persecute you and falsely say all kinds of evil against you because of me. Rejoice and be glad, because great is your reward in heaven, for in the same way they persecuted the prophets who were before you." (Matt 5:11-12)

> "I am sending you out like sheep among wolves. Therefore be as shrewd as snakes and as innocent as doves. Be on your guard; you will be handed over to the local councils and be flogged in the synagogues. On my account you will be brought before governors and kings as witnesses to them and to the Gentiles…
>
> Brother will betray brother to death, and a father his child; children will rebel against their parents and have them put to death. You will be hated by everyone because of me, but the one who stands firm to the end will be saved…
>
> The student is not above the teacher, nor a servant

above his master. It is enough for students to be like their teachers, and servants like their masters. If the head of the house has been called Beelzebul, how much more the members of his household!" (Matt 10:16-18, 21-22, 24-25)

"Then you will be handed over to be persecuted and put to death, and you will be hated by all nations because of me. At that time many will turn away from the faith and will betray and hate each other." (Matt 24:9-10)

To follow Jesus is to take up our cross and die to our sinful selves and find true life in him. But it might also mean that we literally lose our lives because we follow him. It will definitely mean that in some way or another we will suffer difficulty or abuse because we are Christians. This is not just a bad thing from a relative point of view; this really is terrible. The kinds of awful suffering that Christians have experienced and still do experience is outrageous and heart-wrenching. We don't need to hear many stories about the persecuted church before we pray with the saints in Revelation, "How long, Sovereign Lord, holy and true, until you judge the inhabitants of the earth and avenge our blood?" (Rev 6:10)

However, as with any other kind of suffering in this world, this cannot be avoided; it is not optional. In the world as it really is, suffering for the sake of Christ is the good and right thing to do. The suffering itself is truly bad, but the life that leads to this suffering is good and right. There is no other way to live well in the world. To literally lose your life for the sake of the gospel is the best way to live your life, all things

     THE GOOD LIFE IN THE LAST DAYS

considered. Because of this, there is actually a unique kind of glory and delight in suffering for the sake of Christ:

> The apostles left the Sanhedrin, rejoicing because they had been counted worthy of suffering disgrace for the Name. (Acts 5:41)

> Rejoice inasmuch as you participate in the sufferings of Christ, so that you may be overjoyed when his glory is revealed. If you are insulted because of the name of Christ, you are blessed, for the Spirit of glory and of God rests on you… If you suffer as a Christian, do not be ashamed, but praise God that you bear that name. (1 Pet 4:13-14, 16)

The apostle Paul describes his suffering for the sake of the Corinthian church as a glorious experience and manifestation of both the death and resurrection of Jesus in his own body. He says, speaking of himself, "we always carry around in our body the death of Jesus" in suffering, but he is enabled to persevere by the resurrection power of Christ, "so that the life of Jesus may also be revealed in our body" (2 Cor 4:10). And through this suffering Christ brings eternal life to Paul's disciples, so that his suffering is like a death and resurrection for the sake of the church: "So then, death is at work in us, but life is at work in you" (2 Cor 4:12; see also 1:3-7 and 6:3-10)—what a glorious honour![67]

There are complexities and subtleties here. When do we speak up for Christ, and how loudly? When do we flee

---

67  See NT Wright, *The Resurrection of the Son of God,* Society for Promoting Christian Knowledge, London, 2003, pp. 306, 362-3.

persecution and when do we stay put and preach Christ, no matter what the consequences? Such questions require careful reflection and often have more than one right answer. How to make decisions in such situations will be explored in chapters 6, 7 and 8. Still, no matter how we choose to act in the details, "everyone who wants to live a godly life in Christ Jesus will be persecuted" (2 Tim 3:12).

## 'Living as if': Treating this world as temporary and knowing the time is short

We saw in chapter 2 that we find clarity on how to live by noting who people are, where they are and when they are. And I suggested there that the biggest possible perspective on 'when' people are is within God's timetable for all of history. These are the last days, before the return of Christ, the final judgement and then an eternity of joy with Christ, or suffering without him. So a life lived well, will remember that we are in this world, in these last days, face to face with people who are either in Christ or 'in Adam'. Since we know the time we are in, how should we live? This brings us to the passage we have already touched on several times:

> The time is short. From now on those who have wives should live as if they do not; those who mourn, as if they did not; those who are happy, as if they were not; those who buy something, as if it were not theirs to keep; those who use the things of the world, as if not engrossed in them. For this world in its present form is passing away. (1 Cor 7:29-31)

         THE GOOD LIFE IN THE LAST DAYS

What kind of behaviour does Paul have in mind in this passage? It is a very troubling passage on first reading, especially the first item in the list: "those who have wives [or husbands][68] should live as if they do not". I have a strong sense of duty to care for my wife (as she does for me) and it feels so wrong that God's word might command that we should not care for each other well. More than that, I feel strong affection and tenderness towards her (as she does for me) and it hurts to think that God wants us to be aloof from one another. Is marriage merely a vehicle for children, housework and sexual favours? It's hard to reconcile this with my experience—an experience that is itself informed by the gorgeous biblical teaching about marriage in passages like Ephesians 5:22-32.

So what is God saying through the apostle? Clearly it is not that we should all abandon our marriages—see even the teaching of this very chapter:

> The husband should fulfil his marital duty to his wife, and likewise the wife to her husband. The wife does not have authority over her own body but yields it to her husband. In the same way, the husband does not have authority over his own body but yields it to his wife. Do not deprive each other except perhaps by mutual consent and for a time... (1 Cor 7:3-5)

68 It should be said that this does not apply only to husbands and not to wives. This short paragraph has a structured, proverbial style and so to conform to that style has chosen to simply refer to "those who have wives" and not "those who have husbands". However the rest of the chapter is noteworthy for how often it rephrases its advice to men and women in turn (7:3-4, 12-13, 16, 25-27, 32-34). There is no good reason to think that this little proverbial passage was exclusively relevant to men.

> A married man is concerned about the affairs of
> this world—how he can please his wife… a married
> woman is concerned about the affairs of this world—
> how she can please her husband. (vv. 33-34)[69]

Likewise, he is not saying that we should ignore all our emotions, throw away all our property and stop interacting with the things of this world. The key lies in the little word translated into English 'as if'. He does not say "those who have wives, leave them", but "those who have wives live *as if* they do not"; not "those who mourn, cheer up", but "those who mourn *as if* they did not"; not "those who buy something, give it away." The final two examples in the series are perhaps the most helpful in clarifying his meaning: "those who buy something as if it were not theirs to keep; those who use the things of the world, as if not engrossed in them." Here we are not urged to an absolute abandonment of duties and joys associated with worldly things, but a relative disengagement from them, a qualified stance towards them, knowing that they are, in their present form, temporary. This is no justification to neglect your family, suppress your emotions and fail to service your car. This is an extra motivation to hold all such things loosely.

As Martin Luther describes it, we should "not sink too deeply into [the world] either with love and desire or suffering and boredom but should rather behave like guests on earth, using everything for a short time because of need".[70]

---

69  Or consider the stern teaching in 1 Timothy 5:8: "Anyone who does not provide for their relatives, and especially for their own household, has denied the faith and is worse than an unbeliever"!

70  Cited in Thiselton, *Paul's First Letter to the Corinthians,* p. 584.

We are citizens of heaven, aliens and strangers in this world, looking forward to a heavenly country (Phil 3:20; Heb 11:8-10, 13-16; 1 Pet 1:17, 2:11). Calvin describes it in a similar way:

> All things that are connected with the enjoyment of the present life are sacred gifts of God, but we pollute them when we abuse them… We always dream of continuance in the world, for it is owing to this that those things which ought to be helps in passing through it become hindrances to hold us fast… For the man who considers that he is a stranger in the world uses the things of this world as if they were another's… Paul, therefore, directs us to a sober and frugal use of things, such as may not impede or retard our course, but may allow of our always hastening forward toward the goal.[71]

This 'living as if' stance doesn't deny the goodness of this world, nor does it show lack of concern for the people and things of the world; it still treats things as they are with kindness and respect and even delight. This kind of sacrifice is really a subset of the first type of sacrifice we talked about in this chapter: 'sacrificing one good thing for another'. Because of our eager expectation of the new creation and our passionate concern for the preaching of the gospel, we will be less engrossed with the genuinely lovely things and truly noble tasks of this present world. This means that Christians are often more temperate and frugal than we

---

71  John Calvin, *Commentaries on Corinthians,* vol. 1, trans. John Pringle. Accessed from *Christian Classics Ethereal Library* (viewed 24 October 2017): www.ccel.org/ccel/calvin/calcom39.xiv.vii.html

might otherwise be. We are not only wary of the sins of excess—like vanity, laziness, greed and gluttony—but we are also concerned to set our hearts on eternal things.

Don Carson summarizes things well:

> During this period between the [the first and second coming of Christ], Christians must learn to live "as if not": *everything* linked exclusively to an age that is passing must fall under the judgement of God's "as if not". Christians are so linked with the age to come, they so live with eternity's values in view, that the joys and sorrows and realities that are part of this age cannot be allowed to dominate their lives… All is placed under God's "as if not": Christians live with the perspectives of the new age so deeply embedded in their minds and hearts that the foci of this age are held more loosely, "*as if* they do *not*" have permanent validity or ultimate importance—precisely because *they do not!*[72]

## 'Living as if': Treating this world as temporary and knowing the time is short

The series of hard sayings at the end of Luke 9 seem to give some examples of what it might look like to 'live as if' and so are worth considering, to reinforce what we have already seen in 1 Corinthians 7:

**72** DA Carson, *The Sermon on the Mount and His Confrontation with the World: An Exposition of Matthew 5-10,* Global Christian Publishers, Toronto, 1999, pp. 189-90.

As they were walking along the road, a man said to him, "I will follow you wherever you go".

Jesus replied, "Foxes have dens and birds have nests, but the Son of Man has no place to lay his head".

He said to another man, "Follow me".

But he replied, "Lord, first let me go and bury my father".

Jesus said to him "Let the dead bury their own dead, but you go and proclaim the kingdom of God".

Still another said, "I will follow you, Lord; but first let me go back and say goodbye to my family".

Jesus replied, "No-one who puts a hand to the plough and looks back is fit for service in the kingdom of God". (Luke 9:57-62)

The teaching here has similarities to 1 Corinthians 7, but it is important to note a significant difference in context. These encounters take place during Jesus' earthly ministry, as he is on the way to Jerusalem for his crucifixion (Luke 9:51), so they are not directly applicable to all Christians living in the time after his death, resurrection and ascension. We cannot physically follow Jesus in the way that these men could. In fact, even at that time, not everyone who put their faith in Jesus was required to join him on his travels.[73] This means we need to read this passage in its original setting, before drawing out broader principles of application. With that in mind, let's consider each of the three encounters in turn.

73  Schrage, *The Ethics of the New Testament,* pp. 48-51.

*To the first man, Jesus explains the low quality of life he lives as an itinerant evangelist*: "the Son of Man has no place to lay his head". He has set aside the good comforts of a stable life because of the great importance of his message. If anyone wants to travel with him on his mission, they will need to accept the lifestyle that goes with it. Not all those who believed in Jesus joined his travelling party, and not all Christians today need to be itinerant evangelists. But our concern for the kingdom of God ought to shape our quality of life in some way or another too. For the sake of the great thing it is to be involved in Jesus' mission, we will give up other good things, like comfort and stability, when it is necessary to do so. This is not a command for Christians to always avoid buying homes, or good mattresses, but an example of how we might not always be able to, if we make the mission of the Son of Man a high priority.

*The second man is explicitly called by Jesus to physically follow him and this is the context in which his request, and Jesus' surprisingly stern reply must be understood*: "Let the dead bury their own dead, but you go and proclaim the kingdom of God." If he delayed too long, he would either be requiring Jesus to delay his own journey or else be left behind. As Carson writes, "Jesus' concern… is not so much to forbid all who would follow him from attending the funerals of near relatives."[74] Sometimes extenuating circumstances do prevent us from attending to even the most important family obligations. This man has been personally called by God the Son incarnate, to share in his evangelistic mission. Christians

**74** DA Carson, *The Sermon on the Mount and His Confrontation with the World,* p. 180.

should not recklessly apply this episode to systematically neglect family duties in favour of gospel opportunities. But if applied with care and wisdom it might be applied in just this way. Overseas missionary work, for example, has often caused men and women to miss out on many important occasions—both joyous and tragic—in the lives of their close relatives: a painful sacrifice they make for the cause of Christ.

*The third man makes what seems to be a reasonable request,* especially since this story seems to echo the call of Elisha the prophet: "Let me kiss my father and mother goodbye… and then I will come with you" (1 Kgs 19:19-21). Once again it is important to remember that this encounter is about whether and when the man will literally follow Jesus on his way to Jerusalem. In this case it is worth considering whether Jesus is in fact forbidding him from saying goodbye, or just warning against failing to truly make a clean break. The man should be like Elisha who burned his plough, slaughtered his oxen and had a farewell feast. How does this relate to us? Even if we do not have to geographically leave our family for the sake of the gospel, we should still not wistfully long after our former, non-Christian way of life and the worldly expectations of our family members. In particular, before we take on a significant ministry responsibility we should make sure we are not doing so in a fickle manner. We do not need hobby ministers, but single-minded ones, as Paul urges Timothy:

> Join with me in suffering, like a good soldier of Christ Jesus. No-one serving as a soldier gets entangled in civilian affairs, but rather tries to please his command-ing officer. Similarly, anyone who competes as an athlete does not receive the victor's crown except by

competing according to the rules. The hardworking farmer should be the first to receive a share of the crops. (2 Tim 2:3-6)

So we should treat things as temporary because we are in the last days. The self-denial or sacrifice commanded in 1 Corinthians 7 and Luke 9 is not absolute, but relative, because of the time we are in. It is the particular, last days expression of the general principle to love things as they are, where they are and when they are. Treating things as temporary doesn't mean mistreating them, or neglecting them, but simply recognizing that they are temporary and so not becoming so engrossed in them that we lose sight of eternal things.

## Summary

To summarize then, there are five types of suffering, sacrifice or self-denial that we experience in the Christian life:

1. *Sacrificing one good thing for another:* which can be painful, but is not an actual bad or evil thing. It is the natural result of being finite beings in a finite world.
2. *Denying the sinful self:* which is only a sacrifice from the perspective of the sinful self.
3. *Suffering in a fallen world:* which is truly bad but an unavoidable reality for all people, and is experienced in a unique way by Christians.
4. *Suffering for the sake of Christ:* which is truly bad but an unavoidable reality for Christians, and has a unique glory and honour attached to it.

5. *Treating things as temporary and knowing the time is short:* which can be painful but is not an actual bad or evil thing. It is the right way to live in the time that we are in.

To suffer for the sake of Christ and to consciously live in these last days, knowing that the time is short is the right way to live life. It is the best way to live life. And it is actually worth the difficulties and the sorrow that comes with it. It is really worth it.

5

# A THEOLOGY OF SACRIFICE: REALLY GOOD, REALLY REAL, REALLY WORTH IT

In his book *Serving Without Sinking*, John Hindley articulates the felt experience of many keen, ministry-minded Christians:

> When we come to Jesus, He actually seems to increase our burdens. If Jesus is really, finally and ultimately about offering us rest, then it seems strange that He would add to our weariness now. Yet isn't that often how it feels? Have you ever got to the end of the week and wished you had two days to do whatever you wanted? Thought how nice it would be to sleep late *twice* at the weekend? Envied your co-workers who get to lie on a beach when you are off to help at a Christian camp for teenagers? Or totalled up your giving over the year and then thought, as you begin

your 'staycation', of where you could have gone if you'd spent the money you earned on yourself?[75]

Are we missing out if we live God's way? If we get too zealous about Christian stuff, will we live less fulfilling lives? Is this part of the sacrifice of serving Christ in these last days—to live disappointing lives in this present age?

It's hard to really measure in absolute terms whether we are missing out as Christians. How would you measure it? By reported levels of happiness or fulfilment adjusted for statistical accuracy?[76] Is this the best way to measure true joy? And is 'optimal happiness and life satisfaction' a sure-fire way to discover the true 'good life' anyway? I'm not sure how we could measure whether Christians are overall a bit less happy and fulfilled (or a bit *more* happy and fulfilled) in this life than non-Christians. But it doesn't matter, because the Bible doesn't frame things quite like this anyway. You can't really talk about 'the good life' or 'blessing' in abstract terms. Ultimately it is our creator who determines what is truly good and who can tell us how to live our lives as we were created to be. In this chapter, I want to say that dying to self, putting Christ first and treating the things of this world as temporary is the best way to live life. It's really good because it's really real and it's really worth it. As we explored in chapter 3, the right way to live is

**75** John Hindley, *Serving Without Sinking: How to Serve Christ and Keep Your Joy,* Good Book Company, UK, 2014, p. 14.
**76** A few helpful little articles uncovered by a quick Google search: David Sze, 'Measuring Your Happiness Using the Most Important Concept in Positive Psychology, *Huffington Post,* 29 July 2015 (viewed 25 October 2017): www.huffingtonpost.com/david-sze/measuring-your-happiness-_b_7889406.html; and Cristen Conger, 'How Do You Measure Happiness?', *HowStuffWorks* (viewed 25 October 2017): http://science.howstuffworks.com/life/measure-happiness.htm

determined by our place in his creation: who we are, where we are and when we are. Since it is in fact the last days, to live well is to live in the light of this.

## 'Living as if' is really real

To live a life that reflects the fact that "this world in its present form is passing away" and so to not be "engrossed" in the "things of this world" is to live in the world the way it really is. It may be difficult and painful. But it's real. It's not suppressing the truth and making up a world you'd like to believe in, it's not ignoring the bad bits and thinking you can somehow preserve only the good bits.[77] How much better to acknowledge our heavenly Father as the true and living God, to see the world as God's good-but-fallen-creation, to know ourselves as redeemed and destined for glory and to recognize the things of this world are passing away. We have a purpose, we are going somewhere, we are living for something. As Martin Luther King Jnr said, "There are some things so dear, some things so precious, some things so eternally true, that they are worth dying for. And I submit to you that if a man has not discovered something that he will die for, he isn't fit to live."[78]

77 In *Resurrection and Moral Order,* Oliver O'Donovan describes how the sinful human "must create for itself a new order, a fantastic [fantasy] order without objective reality or substance, formed around the new [sinful] orientation of the will, a paradositic [of or related to tradition] imitation of reality which it calls 'my' good" (p. 111).
78 Martin Luther King Jr, 'Speech at the Great March on Detroit, 23 June 1963', *Martin Luther King, Jr. Research Institute,* Stanford University, 2016 (viewed 25 October 2017): http://kingencyclopedia.stanford.edu/encyclopedia/ documentsentry/doc_speech_at_the_great_march_on_detroit/

It is not all for nothing. If you do suffer as a Christian, or go without as a Christian, it is for the best of reasons. You are not ruining the only life you have; you are living your life as part of the ultimate purpose of all things. In the film *The Martian*, stranded astronaut Mark Watney gives a message to be passed on to his parents, in case NASA are unable to rescue him from Mars: "Please tell them… I love what I do and I'm really good at it. And that I'm dying for something big and beautiful and greater than me. Tell them I said I can live with that."[79] This sounds similar to the last written words we have from the apostle Paul:

> For I am already being poured out like a drink offering, and the time for my departure is near. I have fought the good fight, I have finished the race, I have kept the faith. Now there is in store for me the crown of righteousness, which the Lord, the righteous Judge, will award to me on that day. (2 Tim 4:6-8)

What a wonderful way to look back on your life! It was bitter and sometimes sweet, it was hard and sometimes restful, it was full of joy and sorrow, success and failure, heartbreak and bliss. But through it all, I lived for what is good and true. For something even bigger and more beautiful and greater than the human race or space exploration: serving our glorious Lord Jesus Christ.

'Living as if' is really real. But can we say that it is also really good? And what does 'good' mean, anyway?

---

79 'A closer look at… The Martian', *Damaris Media Film Blog,* 14 October 2015 (viewed 25 October 2017): www.filmblog.damaris.org/the-martian/

## What is true blessing?

If we think about how the Bible talks about 'the good life', 'happiness' or 'life satisfaction' then 'blessing' is a very important term. Some translators suggest that 'happy' might be a good English translation of the term[80], but most theologians are rightly concerned that this might reduce the idea to merely what psychologists call 'positive affect': feeling cheerful. Rather, the kind of blessing the Bible celebrates carries with it a full package: the relationship that makes the blessing possible, the many particular blessings that are received, the ability to enjoy the blessing and the duration of the blessing.

*First of all, it is true that good things are blessings*: food, riches, family and so on. If I have these things, I am, in a simple sense, 'blessed'. The blessing promised to Israel if they kept the Sinai covenant is partly described like this:

> All these blessings will come on you and accompany you if you obey the LORD your God:
>
> You will be blessed in the city and blessed in the country.
>
> The fruit of your womb will be blessed, and the crops of your land and the young of your livestock— the calves of your herds and the lambs of your flocks.
>
> Your basket and your kneading trough will be blessed.
>
> You will be blessed when you come in and blessed when you go out. (Deut 28:2-6)

If they were faithful to the covenant, they were promised blessing from God in an abundance of many good, physical

---

80  For example, the Good News translation.

things. Their experience in the promised land would be like a return to the luscious garden of Eden.

*Secondly, the ability to enjoy good things is considered a blessing.* One of the "meaningless" tragedies of Ecclesiastes is the inability to enjoy good things:

> When God gives someone wealth and possessions, and the ability to enjoy them, to accept their lot and be happy in their toil—this is a gift of God. They seldom reflect on the days of their life, because God keeps them occupied with gladness of heart.
>
> I have seen another evil under the sun, and it weighs heavily on mankind: God gives some people wealth, possessions and honour, so that they lack nothing their hearts desire, but God does not grant them the ability to enjoy them, and strangers enjoy them instead. This is meaningless, a grievous evil.
>
> A man may have a hundred children and live many years; yet no matter how long he lives, if he cannot enjoy his prosperity and does not receive a proper burial, I say that a stillborn child is better off than he… even if he lives a thousand years twice over but fails to enjoy his prosperity. Do not all go to the same place? (Eccl 5:19-6:3, 6:6)

The great thing about John Piper's classic *Desiring God* is that it demonstrates that our heavenly Father doesn't simply create us and save us to live rational and moral lives, but lives that find joy in him and all his good gifts.[81] Piper draws

---

81   John Piper, *Desiring God: Meditations of a Christian Hedonist,* rev. edn, Multnomah Books, Colorado Springs, 2011.

   THE GOOD LIFE IN THE LAST DAYS

our attention to the first question of the Westminster Shorter Catechism:

> Q: What is the chief end of man?
>
> A: Man's chief end is to glorify God, and *enjoy him* forever.[82]

While I don't agree with a fair bit of Piper's structuring of the idea of 'Christian Hedonism'[83], the kernel of truth that it is good to delight in God and his gifts is indeed a 'game changer'. True blessing is not just to have lots of good things, but for God to enable us to truly enjoy them.

*Thirdly, the best blessings last.* The comfort we find throughout the psalms is that although the wicked may enjoy many good things now, and perhaps even take great joy and pleasure in them, their blessings do not last. Their pleasure and joy is fleeting, and so it is insubstantial. The righteous enjoy greater blessing, because what they receive from the Lord is a blessing that will truly last.

82 *Westminster Shorter Catechism,* 1647, question 1. Accessed from *The Orthodox Presbyterian Church* (viewed 1 November 2017): www.opc.org/sc.html

83 A few points: 1) I am unconvinced that we are *commanded* to rejoice, I would rather say we are exhorted to rejoice. A verb in the imperative mood is not necessarily a command. 2) I don't think it is true to say that "We glorify God *by* enjoying him". While our joy in God does glorify him, this is not the overarching category for how we glorify him. We also glorify him by obeying him and relying upon him and so on. 3) I disagree with the idea that the one overarching impulse for human activity is 'seeking joy'. Seeking to do the right thing can't easily be collapsed into that. Joy is the wonderful benefit of the Christian life, rather than its primary goal. 4) I am troubled by the claim that we can only please God if we pursue joy. We can please God even if we do not experience joy from time to time, or focus on the pursuit of joy in a particular act. 5) While the term 'hedonism' is used to be helpfully provocative, I think it is more off-putting than illuminating.

Do not fret because of those who are evil
    or be envious of those who do wrong;
for like the grass they will soon wither,
    like green plants they will soon die away…

A little while, and the wicked will be no more;
    though you look for them, they will not be found.
But the meek will inherit the land
    and enjoy peace and prosperity. (Ps 37:1-2, 10-11)

In the end, the psalmists are confident that the blessing of
the righteous is the only blessing that will last and is
therefore the blessing that is truly worth having. Jesus picks
up this idea, even alluding to the psalm just quoted, in the
Beatitudes,

"Blessed are the poor in spirit,
    for theirs is the kingdom of heaven…
Blessed are the meek,
    for they will inherit the earth." (Matt 5:3, 5)

*Finally, it is relationship with God that is the foundational and
supreme blessing.* Often the psalms celebrate the fact that it is
the Lord himself who is the greatest joy and pleasure and
blessing:

I say to the Lord, "You are my Lord;
    apart from you I have no good thing." (Ps 16:2)

I have seen you in the sanctuary
    and beheld your power and your glory.
Because your love is better than life,
    my lips will glorify you.

　　　　THE GOOD LIFE IN THE LAST DAYS

> I will praise you as long as I live,
> and in your name I will lift up my hands.
> I will be satisfied as with the richest of foods;
> with singing lips my mouth will praise you.
> (Ps 63:2-5)

Not only is this recognizing that the Lord is the giver of all good gifts, but that he himself is the greatest gift of all. He is the first pleasure to delight in, the source of true satisfaction.

True blessing, then, is the 'full package' of all these things: peace with God, and the ability to enjoy all the good things he gives in a lasting way. This 'full package' vision of blessing means that the psalmists can speak in curious, almost contradictory ways. They can speak confidently about the righteous never suffering in the very same psalms that also lament the suffering of the righteous! For example, in a psalm about the suffering of King David, that speaks often about the troubles, poverty and affliction of the righteous, we read:

> Taste and see that the LORD is good;
> blessed is the one who takes refuge in him.
> Fear the LORD, you his holy people,
> for those who fear him lack nothing…
>
> Whoever of you loves life
> and desires to see many good days,
> keep your tongue from evil
> and your lips from telling lies.
> Turn from evil and do good;
> seek peace and pursue it. (Ps 34:8-9, 12-14)

The blessing people have in God is so good and the hope they have in him is so sure, that when they experience blessing and joy in the Lord, they are experiencing things the way things should be—and one day will be. When they experience suffering while faithfully serving God, they entrust themselves to him, confident that it won't last. Although there isn't a clear theology of the final judgement and renewal of all things in the psalms, this theme ultimately points in that direction: to a confidence that justice will be fully done and blessing for God's people will be full and unceasing.

Blessing then, is more than simply enjoying good things. We need to know God's will and God's purposes to truly know what blessings are ultimately worth having.


## Blessing in the Christian life

The psalmists appeal to the Lord in the midst of their suffering and confidently ask for blessing. In the life, death and resurrection of Jesus we see that this was a pattern of suffering-before-blessing, which foreshadows what the great suffering king Jesus would experience. So Jesus experiences the suffering of the psalms (for example John 13:18 and 19:24) and their hope of blessing is fulfilled in him too (for example Luke 23:46 and Acts 2:21-32).

What does that mean for us as Christians? *Firstly, we are blessed because of Jesus' death for us.* Jesus' suffering had greater meaning than that of the psalmists, because he suffered on behalf of his people, as a substitutionary sacrifice.[84]

---

84 It's curious on first reading how many psalms about the personal suffering of the king end not just with hope for personal blessing for the king, but expectation of blessings for God's people, God's land and even the whole world (e.g. Pss 22:25-31, 51:18-19, 69:34-36). This is because when God's king is rescued and blessed he can bring blessing to those he rules over. Unlike Jesus, however, their suffering itself is not a mechanism that brings blessing to others.

 THE GOOD LIFE IN THE LAST DAYS

Because our king has suffered for us and has now been blessed in his resurrection and ascension, we enjoy the great blessings that flow from this. In particular, the blessing of peace with God, the guarantee of eternal blessings and the ability to enjoy these blessings are all ours by faith in the Lord Jesus Christ (see Romans 5:1-11). We have the best blessings of all in Christ!

*Secondly, just as the pattern for Christ was suffering before glory, so also for Christians, we expect to suffer in this life, with the sure hope of eternal blessing in the age to come.* This is our Father's good purpose, so we can rejoice in the strange blessing it is to suffer for the sake of Christ and grow in our faith through suffering, as we explored in chapter 4. As Peter writes:

> To this you were called, because Christ suffered for you, leaving you an example, that you should follow in his steps.
>
> "He committed no sin,
>     and no deceit was found in his mouth."
>
> When they hurled their insults at him, he did not retaliate; when he suffered, he made no threats. Instead, he entrusted himself to him who judges justly. (1 Pet 2:21-23)

Because true blessing is a 'full package', Christians look for the blessing that comes from a right relationship with God. And since he has revealed to us that these are the last days, we want to enjoy blessings in line with being a part of his purposes: even though this brings with it struggling and hardship. The promises of physical blessing, like those given to Israel in the Sinai covenant, are not offered to Christians in this life, as if the normal Christian life will be one of physical health, economic prosperity and political triumph. Rather the pattern of the Christian life, like that of Christ's, is spiritual blessing together with physical suffering in this life, followed by physical blessing at the final resurrection.

*Thirdly, this doesn't mean we won't ever enjoy good things in this life, or that we shouldn't.* In a few places, Psalms is quoted to talk about the physical blessing that Christians can enjoy in this life. In 2 Corinthians 9, Paul quotes Psalm 112 and applies it to Christians:

> And God is able to bless you abundantly, so that in all things at all times, having all that you need, you will abound in every good work. As it is written:
>
> > "They have freely scattered their gifts to the poor;
> >     their righteousness endures for ever."
>
> Now he who supplies seed to the sower and bread for food will also supply and increase your store of seed and will enlarge the harvest of your righteousness. You will be enriched in every way so that you can be generous on every occasion, and through us your generosity will result in thanksgiving to God. (2 Cor 9:8-11)

Christians can normally expect to receive good gifts from God—both physical and spiritual—that we can use in generous service of his kingdom and love of others. In the same way, the apostle Peter quotes the promise of blessing found in Psalm 34, reassuring his readers "Who is going to harm you if you are eager to do good?" (1 Pet 3:9-13). The blessing

  THE GOOD LIFE IN THE LAST DAYS

of the psalm still applies to Christians, according to Peter, and this remains true even though, as Peter and his readers know too well, Christians often suffer all kinds of trials. Straight after suggesting that no harm will come to them, Peter goes on to say, "But even if you should suffer for what is right, you are blessed" (3:14).

It is true that the new covenant doesn't have the same promise of abundant physical blessing in this life that the Sinai covenant had. But even in the 'last days' we find ourselves in, the blessing we have in God is so good and the hope we have in him is so sure, that when we experience any blessing and joy from the Lord, we are experiencing things the way they should be—and one day will be. It is good and fitting to suffer now, but this is not because suffering itself is good, but because this is the right thing in the last days. It is good and fitting for us to use the things of this world lightly, not because the things of this world are bad, but because this world in its present form is passing away. When we suffer and do without, we are recognizing that this world is fallen, cursed and passing away. But when we enjoy good things, we are recognizing that this fallen, temporary world is still God's creation and will one day be made new and enjoyed more wonderfully than Adam and Eve could ever have done.[85]

---

85 "The great difference between Stoic and Christian renunciation is this: for the Stoic, what is renounced is, if rightly renounced… not part of the good. For the Christian, what is renounced is thereby affirmed as good—both in the sense that the renunciation would lose its meaning if the thing were indifferent and in the sense that the renunciation is in furtherance of God's will, which precisely affirms the goodness of the kinds of things renounced: health, freedom, life. Paradoxically, Christian renunciation is an affirmation of the goodness of what is renounced.

…In the Christian perspective… the loss is a breach in the integrity of the good. That is why Christianity requires an [end time] perspective of the restoral of that integrity" (Taylor, *Sources of Self,* p. 219).

## Don't envy the world

The blessed life, the *true*, blessed life is lived serving the Lord. There's no 'better life' out there somehow, that the non-Christians have, and that you're missing out on. In the real world as it actually is, this is the best option. We need to repent of entertaining that kind of twisted, resentful Christian envy of the world, where we think "If I weren't a Christian I'd be having so much more fun… but oh well, I'm a Christian."

Would a life lived for nothing greater than holidays and materialism and selfish desire be a better life? Living for nothing greater or more valuable than pleasure, experience, power and ambition? Is it not the wretched despair of "let us eat and drink, for tomorrow we die" (Isa 22:13)? As Ecclesiastes vividly describes:

Again I saw something meaningless under the sun:

> There was a man all alone;
> he had neither son nor brother.
> There was no end to his toil,
> yet his eyes were not content with his wealth.
> "For whom am I toiling," he asked,
> "and why am I depriving myself of enjoyment?"
> This too is meaningless—
> a miserable business! (Eccl 4:7-8)

Dying to our sinful self, tearing down our pathetic idols and worshipping the true and living God is a better way to live. It's not good to live in sin and idolatry and folly and selfishness—that's a miserable and tragic way to live. Peter calls it the "empty way of life handed down to you from your ancestors" (1 Pet 1:18) and Paul asks us "What benefit did you reap at that time from the things you are now ashamed of? Those things result in death!" (Rom 6:21). Renouncing the sinful life is actually the path to true freedom.

Much suffering is just part of living in God's world. Everyone, Christian and non-Christian, misses out on things; you can't do everything there is to do. And no-one, Christian or non-Christian, can avoid all sin, suffering and sickness. And ultimately none of us can buy our way out of the grave:

> No-one can redeem the life of another
> or give to God a ransom for them—
> the ransom for a life is costly,
> no payment is ever enough—
> so that they should live on for ever
> and not see decay. (Ps 49:7-9)

Everyone suffers in a fallen world. Non-Christians, even the rich and beautiful ones, struggle and sacrifice and experience great tragedy. All of us, and everyone that we love, will one day return to dust. In that sense, envying the world is naïve. The wise learn to "number our days", knowing that they "may come to seventy years, or eighty, if our strength endures" (Ps 90:10, 12).

Because Christians understand the Fall, we expect suffering in this life, and so we are not caught by surprise when it comes our way. Because we have the hope of eternal life, we do not try to focus on making this life as comfortable as possible. This might mean that a Christian will not put quite as much energy into solving their problems of sickness or poverty or unhappiness as they would have done if their hope was only for this life. They might pursue a path of contentment through difficulty, which tolerates rather than tries to remove all discomfort. The surprising thing might be that in doing this, they might end up increasing their overall quality of life by being freed from an anxious, burdensome and disappointing fixation on 'solving' all their problems in this life.[86] We should not envy those who are caught in the futile attempt to return to Eden.

Not only is envying the world naïve, it is also short-sighted.

## 'Living as if' is really worth it

Living for Christ, in the light of the last days and orienting my life for eternity, means I turn away from many short-term pleasures and joys—even good, godly pleasures. But this is not giving up on the good for the bad, it is giving up the good for the better. Wolfgang Schrage observes that not all the passages that speak about giving up things, are stern challenges. For example, the parable of the treasure in the field speaks of selling everything you own as an act of joy (Matthew 13:44). Schrage explains, "The kingdom of God… has already irrupted into the present as a joyfully acknowledged discovery, as something that even now brings salvation, joy, and direction."[87]

And it is really worth it. Ultimately, as Joe Rigney reminds us:

There is a death and resurrection movement in all of our self-denial. We lose our life in order to save it. We

---

86  Thanks to my wife Nikki for this insight.
87  Schrage, *The Ethics of the New Testament,* pp. 29-30.

                    THE GOOD LIFE IN THE LAST DAYS

forfeit the world that we might gain ourselves. We willingly suffer daily death that we might, like Christ, be triumphantly raised from the dead.[88]

Rigney goes on to point out how so many of the passages where we are urged to suffer or give up something in this life, also promise great blessing and reward. Our Lord is ultimately interested in our good, not merely our obedience. We are giving up good things for better things. Consider just one example:

> Then Peter spoke up, "We have left everything to follow you!"
>
> "Truly I tell you," Jesus replied, "no-one who has left home or brothers or sisters or mother or father or children or fields for me and the gospel will fail to receive a hundred times as much in this present age: homes, brothers, sisters, mothers, children and fields —along with persecutions—and in the age to come eternal life." (Mark 10:28-30)

We need to keep on teaching our minds and stirring our imaginations to see the world the way God sees it. It is good to be a Christian. To live the full, zealous, devout, all-in, passionate Christian life. It's a good way to love your spouse and live your lives together. It's a good way to raise your kids and give them all the good things that are actually worth having. It's the best way to get the most out of life in the world that we live in, in the time in history we find ourselves. Yes, it will be hard and painful at times, but, as 1 Corinthians

**88**  Rigney, *The Things of Earth,* p. 180.

7:30 teaches us, our emotional states should not dominate our lives either. Martyrdom is not a tragic end to a life, diverting your career into Christian ministry is not a waste of talent, investing free time in teaching Sunday School and disposable income into giving to missionaries is not a pathetic life choice. At the climax of 1 Corinthians 15, where Paul speaks at length about the resurrection of the dead he writes:

> Listen, I tell you a mystery: We will not all sleep, but we will all be changed—in a flash, in the twinkling of an eye, at the last trumpet. For the trumpet will sound, the dead will be raised imperishable, and we will be changed… When the perishable has been clothed with the imperishable, and the mortal with immortality, then the saying that is written will come true: "Death has been swallowed up in victory."
>
> > "Where, O death, is your victory?
> > Where, O death, is your sting?"
>
> …Therefore, my dear brothers and sisters, stand firm. Let nothing move you. Always give yourselves fully to the work of the Lord, because you know that your labour in the Lord is not in vain. (vv. 51-52, 54-55, 58)

This is truly the good life! And in the end it really will be wonderfully, eternally worth it.

**6**

# PUTTING IT INTO PRACTICE: THE REALITIES OF LIFE

Sincere, zealous and devout Christians can experience guilt for strange things. In the introduction of his book, *The Things of Earth: Treasuring God by Enjoying His Gifts*, Joe Rigney gives a series of great examples:

> Katherine… worries that she doesn't read her Bible enough. No matter how long her devotions are, the low-grade guilt seems to stay. After all, doesn't the Bible say to meditate on it day and night and to pray without ceasing?

> God used colon cancer to shake Bob loose and draw him to himself. Bob now wonders whether he can enjoy his hobbies like he once did. After all, he doesn't want to waste his life.

> Abby… [has] been worried she loves her fiancé, Dan, too much. She doesn't quite know what 'too much'

means, but whenever she's with him, her heart leaps, and then she immediately feels a sense of guilt.

Sarah knows that her mom is in heaven with Jesus… but [she] still cries almost every night. What's worse, she's started to feel guilty for her grief because she wonders whether God disapproves of the depth of her pain.[89]

There's nothing wrong with guilt in and of itself. Appropriate and proportional guilt is like pain, it alerts us to a danger in order to keep us safe. Guilt is like moral pain, and when it alerts us to genuine evil it drives us away from sin to repentance and faith in God. Even misplaced guilt can have something noble in it. In all the examples above, there is a wonderful desire to honour God and do what is right which is commendable. If we were lawless then life would be a lot less complicated and we'd feel less guilt. There's nothing wrong with guilt, but false and exaggerated guilt is pointless and crippling: it doesn't give God more glory, it doesn't make us more godly and it definitely doesn't give us more joy!

In the next three chapters we are going to explore how to apply the insights of this book to the details of our lives and decisions. How should we serve Christ wholeheartedly, and hold the things of this world loosely, knowing the time is short? It is my hope that being clearer on how to obey the 'hard sayings' of the New Testament will both challenge us with healthy guilt and free us from unhealthy guilt. As we will see, God challenges us but he also counsels us. He pushes us out of our comfort zone and questions the normal, sensible

---

89 Rigney, *The Things of Earth*, pp. 19-20.

   THE GOOD LIFE IN THE LAST DAYS

option. But he also helps us apply these grand ideals to our weakness and tiredness, to our mix of gifts and passions, to our mess of commitments and duties.

We are particularly going to focus on the long, rich and rewarding chapter 7 of 1 Corinthians. This is the chapter where Paul urges the Corinthians to 'live as if' they were not engrossed in the things of this world because it is passing away. That exhortation is part of a section in which Paul speaks to them about marriage and singleness. He corrects their absolute declaration that "it is good for a man not to have sexual relations with a woman" (v. 1)[90], by talking about the advantages of marriage and the godly duties married couples have to one another. But he also strongly commends singleness, and provides reasons why those who are single in the Corinthian church should seriously consider staying single. The decision to stay single is a decision made because "the time is short" and "this world in its present form is passing away", it is one practical 'application' of this truth. So as we follow Paul's reasoning in 1 Corinthians 7, we can learn how to make decisions in the last days. What must we do? What might we do? What should we feel guilty about and what shouldn't we feel guilty about? How do we decide? Paul gives three perspectives in this chapter:

- Realism not idealism
- Different gifts but not different classes of Christian
- Contentment with the circumstances of your calling

90 In their commentary *The First Letter to the Corinthians,* Roy Ciampa and Brian Rosner argue from an extensive study of the expression that this means "It is good for a man not to use a woman for sexual gratification" or "it is good for a man not to have sex with a woman for the sake of pleasure" (Eerdmans, Grand Rapids, MI, 2010, p. 274).

## Realism not idealism

It's interesting to note an assumption that Paul brings to the whole discussion, a stance of realism about the limited capacity of individual Christians. God doesn't speak to us with the simplistic logic: "If you *really* believed you would…" When we think this way, we can tend to look down on others for not being as sacrificial as we are, or kick ourselves in despair for failing to meet our own idealistic standards: clearly we don't *really* believe. Paul's realism is quite surprising by contrast:

- Paul quotes the Corinthian ideal: "It is good for a man not to have sexual relations with a woman" (v. 1)… but then concedes "But since sexual immorality is occurring, each man should have sexual relations with his own wife, and each woman with her own husband. The husband should fulfil his marital duty to his wife, and likewise the wife to her husband" (vv. 2-3).

- He speaks of married couples withholding from sexual relations "so that you may devote yourselves to prayer" (v. 5a)… but then advises "come together again so that Satan will not tempt you because of your lack of self-control" (v. 5b).

- Speaking "to the unmarried and the widows" he says: "it is good for them to stay unmarried, as I do" (v. 8)… but immediately goes on to say, "But if they cannot control themselves, they should marry, for it is better to marry than to burn with passion" (v. 9).

As God speaks through his apostle, he is sensitive to the realities of human desires and limitations. He makes allowances for them. Because God's great interest is in godliness in whatever form it might take, rather than an idealistic, sacrificial lifestyle in and of itself. Garland points out the irony of the Corinthian approach of high ideals:

> Paul may seem to imply the only value of conjugal love is to avert fornication, we must remember that he is reacting to a particular context in which persons are attempting to become asexual. He is not writing a theology of marriage or sexuality. Some Corinthians may think that by renouncing worldly pleasures they will be able to rise to new spiritual heights. Paul demurs. He sees them entering territory that will only lead to their moral downfall.[91]

A very similar piece of counsel is found in 1 Timothy 5:

> As for younger widows… when their sensual desires overcome their dedication to Christ, they want to marry… Besides, they get into the habit of being idle and going about from house to house. And not only do they become idlers, but also busybodies who talk nonsense, saying things they ought not to. So I counsel younger widows to marry, to have children, to manage their homes and to give the enemy no opportunity for slander. (vv. 11, 13-14)

Here, alongside the desire to marry is the inability to effectively use their free time for the gospel and good deeds. This is not to say that all young widows (or widowers) would be unable to use extra free time well, any more than it is

---

91 David E Garland, *1 Corinthians,* Baker Academic, Grand Rapids, MI, 2003, p. 257.

saying that the "sensual desires" of all young widows and widowers would "overcome their dedication to Christ [so that they would] want to marry". It is a generalisation. The idealism that says if we could free up every Christian from regular work they would give more time to gospel ministry does not entirely match reality.

What is true of the ideal of singleness might be true of other possible decisions we might make because of the gospel: a high level of hospitality in the home, welcoming foster children or live-in guests; a lifestyle of extreme minimalist frugality; moving to Yemen to preach the gospel. If we *really* believed the realities of the gospel should we all do things like this? But the realities of human experience do not match this idealism. What for one person is stretching, challenging but do-able is for another person draining and overwhelming. For reasons of physical and emotional makeup, upbringing and spiritual giftedness, not all of us can or will live the Christian life in the same way.

This realism principle can be abused, however. For sin is still sin, and it is never excusable or justifiable, even when it is provoked or inflamed by circumstances. Realism about human desire can enable the Christian community to adopt an attitude to marriage that can help prevent unnecessary temptation. But often a Christian may really want to marry, but for whatever reason has not found a partner. In such circumstances, they must resist the temptation to sexual immorality, even though it is difficult. Likewise, in the Lord's mysterious purposes, he may place us under "great pressure, far beyond our ability to endure" (2 Cor 1:8). Even in such circumstances we must seek to serve the Lord, "not rely[ing] on ourselves but on God, who raises the dead" (v. 9).

 THE GOOD LIFE IN THE LAST DAYS

Realism, not idealism, is our first principle. And it appears in 1 Corinthians 7, not just as a warning against an idealistic embracing of the single life. It also warns against any sentimental idealism about the joys of married life:

> I wish that all of you were as I am… Now to the unmarried and the widows I say: It is good for them to stay unmarried, as I do. (vv. 7-8)

> Now about virgins… Because of the present crisis, I think that it is good for a man to remain as he is… Are you free from such a commitment? Do not look for a wife… Those who marry will face many troubles in this life, and I want to spare you this. (vv. 25-28)

> I would like you to be free from concern. An unmarried man is concerned about the Lord's affairs—how he can please the Lord. But a married man is concerned about the affairs of this world—how he can please his wife—and his interests are divided. An unmarried woman or virgin is concerned about the Lord's affairs: Her aim is to be devoted to the Lord in both body and spirit. But a married woman is concerned about the affairs of this world—how she can please her husband. I am saying this for your own good, not to restrict you, but that you may live in a right way in undivided devotion to the Lord. (vv. 32-35)

> So then, he who marries the virgin does right, but he who does not marry her does better.
>
> A woman is bound to her husband as long as he lives. But if her husband dies, she is free to marry anyone she wishes, but he must belong to the Lord. In

> my judgement, she is happier if she stays as she is—and
> I think that I too have the Spirit of God. (vv. 38-40)

We can buy the lie that as long as we find the 'right person' then marriage will be wonderful and easy: one unceasingly joyous partnership, serving God, raising children and doing ministry. Some have observed that marriage and family often have a distorted value and centrality in contemporary Christian circles, that is more the result of our culture than the Scriptures.[92] By contrast, 1 Corinthians is not only realistic, but seems decidedly *pessimistic* about marriage!

This does not deny the fact that marriage provides pleasures of many kinds (Song of Songs), and a solution to the "not good" of aloneness (Gen 2:18-25), that marriage is the fitting context for raising godly offspring (Mal 2:15)[93] and the founding of a new family and home from which hospitality can be practised and the gospel advanced.[94] In fact marriage is such a good thing that it was created to be a

---

**92** Rodney Clapp in *Families at the Crossroads: Beyond Traditional and Modern Options* writes, "We must resist the hasty and careless blurring of such words as *traditional*, *natural* and *biblical*. Such blurring has created the widespread impression that those who would question aspects of the industrial, middle-class family are disputing Scripture and departing from a way of family that is thousands of years old, even based on the order of nature itself" (IVP, Downers Grove, IL, 1993, p. 16). See also Ash, *Marriage: Sex in the Service of God*, pp. 127-9.

**93** In fact Christopher Ash argues that a fundamental reason it was "not good for man to be alone" was that he would be unable to "fill the earth and subdue it" without a "suitable helper" to help "be fruitful and multiply, fill the earth and subdue it" (*Marriage: Sex in the Service of God*, pp. 116-22). I think Ash rightly helps us see that children are a key part of marriage, but it seems to me that he overstates the case at many points. For example, I believe that marriage is also one of the ways our creator provides companionship to relieve us of the experience of 'loneliness'.

**94** A harder concept to show from a single Bible passage! In marriage the man and woman "leave" their parents to become a new "one flesh" union (Gen 2:25) and are then families and households which are treated as 'units' in the community.

pattern of Christ and the church (Eph 5:22-32). And so it remains true that most Christians will marry, and that marriage will be a common feature in the life of the church in this age.

While this is all true, 1 Corinthians helpfully challenges us: does a man *need* a wife to live a meaningful life? Does a woman *need* a husband to be a whole human being? Can we only fully serve God if we are married? 1 Corinthians is clear. The answer is no.

Why is singleness to be preferred? *Firstly, because of the "many troubles" that marriage brings* (v. 28). It is difficult to know exactly what Paul might be referring to in the first place. Perhaps it is the burden of care for your partner and children that adds extra anxiety especially in times of crisis (v. 26)? Surely it can also include the many troubles, small and great, that living together brings: irritations, quarrels and serious conflicts. As Stanley Hauerwas provocatively says, "You always marry the wrong person"[95]—there is no soulmate with whom marriage is easy and trouble free. We must not adopt an idealistic picture of married life. Even in the way we talk about marriage in church, we should beware of always commending the ideal of 'the happy marriage' and never giving realistic advice on how to "do unhappy marriages Christianly".[96]

*The second reason Paul commends singleness is because marriage divides our attention.* The value of singleness in

---

95 Stanley Hauerwas, 'The Radical Hope in the Annunciation: Why Both Single and Married Christians Welcome Children (1998)' in John Berkman and Michael Cartwright (eds), *The Hauerwas Reader,* Duke University Press, Durham, NI, 2001, p. 513. He also says that the opposite is true: "You always marry the right person", since his point is that we need to be realistic about whomever we marry.

96 I first heard this from Michael Jensen in online dialogue in 2010.

1 Corinthians 7 is that it is practical and strategic, as Paul explains:

> An unmarried man is concerned about the Lord's affairs—how he can please the Lord. But a married man is concerned about the affairs of this world—how he can please his wife—and his interests are divided. An unmarried woman or virgin is concerned about the Lord's affairs: Her aim is to be devoted to the Lord in both body and spirit. But a married woman is concerned about the affairs of this world—how she can please her husband. (vv. 32-34)

Singleness gives the possibility for more time and "undivided devotion" to be given to "the Lord's affairs".[97] In chapter 3, I answered the objection that this seems to deny that we serve the Lord in every area of our lives, including our marriages. There I argued that Paul is speaking comparatively rather than absolutely. When seen in comparison to listening to God's word, praying to God and speaking his word to others, the things of this world "grow strangely dim" as the hymn by Helen Lemmel says.[98] The single Christian has the opportunity to focus on a narrower group of activities that are more

---

**97**  This is a general observation but depends on many cultural and contextual factors. A few examples: 1) A single person with significant practical needs might be better off in the supporting context of a marriage. 2) In the modern world, where communities are transient and more individualistic, a single person has a great deal of shopping, cooking, cleaning and personal administration to manage all on their own, with no division of labour that marriage affords. 3) For the same reasons of transience and individualism, if a single person lives alone, they might feel a lack of 'emotional morale'. 4) Lastly, because of modern contraception, a married couple can have a long period of childlessness, which dramatically lessens the demands of family life, while maximizing division of labour.

**98**  Helen H Lemmel, 'Turn Your Eyes Upon Jesus', 1922.

          THE GOOD LIFE IN THE LAST DAYS

directly concerned with God's word and work—what is called "the work of the Lord" in 1 Corinthians 15:58. There is an intriguing parallel teaching in the gospel of Matthew, where Jesus is also speaking about marriage:

> "I tell you that anyone who divorces his wife, except for sexual immorality, and marries another woman commits adultery."
>
> The disciples said to him, "If this is the situation between a husband and wife, it is better not to marry."
>
> Jesus replied, "Not everyone can accept this word, but only those to whom it has been given. For there are eunuchs who were born that way, and there are eunuchs who have been made eunuchs by others—and there are those who choose to live like eunuchs for the sake of the kingdom of heaven. The one who can accept this should accept it." (Matt 19:9-12)

Singleness can give a peculiar advantage "for the sake of the kingdom of heaven". In *The Wife Drought*, Australian journalist Annabel Crabb explores this from a non-Christian point of view: marriage and children dramatically distract women in particular from other kinds of work outside the home:

> The brutal truth is that childlessness is still probably the biggest natural advantage a woman can give herself in terms of dealing with the demands of a successful career in federal politics.[99]

So also for the "work of the Lord". When you are single you can potentially just study more, disciple more, pray more

---

99 Annabel Crabb, *The Wife Drought: Why Women Need Wives, and Men Need Lives,* Ebury Press, North Sydney, 2014, p. 202.

and travel more for the kingdom of God.[100] In arguing in this way, Paul is surprisingly realistic about the limitations of married life, when it comes to gospel ministry. If we look at this life as a part of this present age, there remains a kind of 'normality' about married life; but if we look at this life as the last days, where the age to come has already dawned, then there is another sense in which the single life should be embraced as more 'normal' in a whole new way.

## With different gifts not different classes

We are to serve Christ in these last days with realism not idealism. And part of that realism is recognizing that each Christian is different, and this is a good thing. What is true in all of creation is true of the church. We are different from each other and so we will serve Christ in different ways. In the discussion of singleness Paul recognizes this, "I wish that all of you were as I am. But each of you has your own gift from God; one has this gift, another has that" (1 Cor 7:7). He unpacks the idea of "gifts"—which he also called "service" and "workings" later on in the same letter:

> There are different kinds of gifts, but the same Spirit distributes them. There are different kinds of service, but the same Lord. There are different kinds of working, but in all of them and in everyone it is the same God at work.
>
> Now to each one the manifestation of the Spirit is

---

**100** A similar practical logic commends paying Christian teachers to free them up to give themselves to "prayer and the ministry of the word" (Acts 6:1-7, 18:1-5; 1 Cor 9:4-12; 1 Tim 5:17-18).

   THE GOOD LIFE IN THE LAST DAYS

given for the common good. To one there is given through the Spirit a message of wisdom, to another a message of knowledge by means of the same Spirit, to another faith by the same Spirit, to another gifts of healing by that one Spirit, to another miraculous powers, to another prophecy, to another distinguishing between spirits, to another speaking in different kinds of tongues, and to still another the interpretation of tongues. All these are the work of one and the same Spirit, and he distributes them to each one, just as he determines.

Just as a body, though one, has many parts, but all its many parts form one body, so it is with Christ. For we were all baptised by one Spirit so as to form one body—whether Jews or Gentiles, slave or free—and we were all given the one Spirit to drink. Even so the body is not made up of one part but of many…

In fact God has placed the parts in the body, every one of them, just as he wanted them to be. If they were all one part, where would the body be? As it is, there are many parts, but one body. (1 Cor 12:4-14, 18-20)

Not everyone is a preacher, not everyone chooses the long-term single life,[101] not everyone is equally passionate about

---

[101]   It is hard to be precise about what Paul means by the "gift" of singleness. I believe it is more than just the state of being single, but a desire and ability to live the single life without succumbing to temptation (see also Thiselton, *1 Corinthians,* pp. 513-14 and Ciampa and Rosner, *1 Corinthians,* pp. 285-6). This is different to the broader sense in which we might find ourselves called to circumstances for which we don't feel especially "gifted", whether unwanted singleness, ministry responsibility or something else (see discussion of the realism principle earlier in this chapter under 'Realism not idealism').

clean water projects in the developing world. We are different. And that is God's good design. He has "placed the parts in the body... just as he wanted them to be" with all our diversity and limitations.

Even if we wanted to, we could not do every possible good thing. Oliver O'Donovan describes three different Christian women:

> Here is a courageous woman who has lived out her life in the slums working for the socially disabled. Here is another of great family-loyalty, who has brought up her children with devotion and has been a rock of support to her kin and community. And here is a third, who has given her energies to an intellectual quest which she has pursued with integrity and self-discipline.[102]

Each is doing good deeds for the glory of God. But it is very difficult for one woman to live all three of these lives in equal measure—that would possibly lead to depression, guilt and exhaustion for most. That limitation is not a failure, any more than the variation is a problem. We might mourn the missed opportunities of another possible life, and this mourning can be very strong and even overwhelming at times; the longing to have children of your own can be a very deep pain, so also the sense of being different from some common or supposedly ideal pattern of life. But as we explored in chapter 4, this is not an evil, cursed thing; rather it is a case of mourning the loss of one good thing for another. If we really affirmed, acknowledged, celebrated and dignified the many different patterns of the Christian life, perhaps an

102  O'Donovan, *Resurrection and Moral Order,* p. 219.

                              THE GOOD LIFE IN THE LAST DAYS

unnecessary edge would be taken off this grief?

We must be clear that these are different gifts, not different classes of Christian—we are all "one body" in Christ Jesus and we have all received the same Spirit (v. 13). Fundamentally we are also all living the same Christian life: loving God with all our heart and mind and soul and strength, and loving our neighbour as ourselves; we are simply expressing it in different ways. That is what the famous passage in 1 Corinthians 13 is all about, that love is more important than gifts:

> If I speak in the tongues of men or of angels, but do not have love, I am only a resounding gong or a clanging cymbal. If I have the gift of prophecy and can fathom all mysteries and all knowledge, and if I have a faith that can move mountains, but do not have love, I am nothing. If I give all I possess to the poor and give over my body to hardship that I may boast, but do not have love, I gain nothing. (vv. 1-3)

Love is valuable in and of itself. By contrast, the various gifts have no intrinsic value, as if the single woman or the man who talks in different kinds of languages were living a higher class of Christian life which glorifies God more fully. The value of gifts is practical and strategic, not moral or spiritual.

The devout, zealous, sacrificial Christian life will look different in each one of us: one of us will preach to thousands; another will earn great wealth and give generously; another will spend their time with the mentally disabled or chronically ill; another will be treasurer for the parish council; another will be a nurse in a hospital in South Sudan; another will connect into rich networks of non-Christian acquaintances and seek to share their faith, another will be patient and prayerful and full of hope despite severe physical suffering; another will be a church planter on the Gold Coast; another will be a member of parliament; still another will be a hard worker, faithful growth group member, thoughtful voter, loving friend and church member who will vote in congregational meetings year after year in favour of changes that advance the gospel at their personal inconvenience. All these lives are lived for the Lord, and all can be deeply concerned for the cause of the gospel. As Kevin DeYoung and Greg Gilbert imagine an older, experienced pastor saying to a young, idealistic urban church planter:

> Don't confuse opportunities and responsibilities. Just because we *can* doesn't mean we *have* to… Don't swing for the fences and try to convince them that they must do [this or that ministry] or else…
>
> People are called to different things. Their consciences are pricked in different ways. So don't expect everyone to be into whatever you're into, or against everything you're against. I remember C. S. Lewis said something like "One of the marks of a certain type of bad man is that he cannot give up a thing himself without wanting everyone else to give it up". What I'm saying is that if you take every last one of your convictions and all your idealistic passions and lay it over your whole congregation you'll wear them out or tear them up.[103]

Sometimes those in Christian leadership speak in a simplistic way of 'letting people off the hook'. For example, if we

---

**103**  DeYoung and Gilbert, *Mission of the Church*, p. 260.

        THE GOOD LIFE IN THE LAST DAYS

don't urge young men and women to do paid Christian leadership we are 'letting them off the hook'. The problem with this stance is that *firstly it wrongly assumes there is a hook that all Christians should be on to begin with!* If God's word does not lay the command of working full-time in word ministry on all Christians, then leaders have no right to do so. It is right to exhort and inspire, as Paul does in many and varied ways throughout 1 Corinthians 7 about the benefits of singleness. So it is true to say that leaders must not 'let people off the hook' of seriously considering such things. However, like the apostle Paul, they must be clear when they do not have the authority to issue a command.

*Secondly, talk about 'letting people off the hook' betrays a lack of trust that God's Spirit is at work in the conscience of each believer.* The 'hook mentality' suggests that Christian leaders have a clear vision of what is good and right, whereas all other Christians are mainly lazy, worldly and evasive. Of course, leaders do sometimes need to "warn those who are idle and disruptive" but they also need to "encourage the disheartened, help the weak, be patient with everyone" (1 Thess 5:14). God's Spirit dwells in every believer, leading them into godliness, forming Christ in them, willing and acting according to his good purpose. Leaders do well to honour the spiritual sincerity of our fellow brothers and sisters in Christ.

Thirdly it assumes that paid Christian ministry is the uniquely hard and sacrificial path. Being a pastor is hard, but so is being a high school teacher. Personal evangelism is hard, but so is being on the set up and pack down roster. Rather than thinking in simple black-and-white terms of being sacrificial or being soft, we need to urge one another to be sacrificial according to gifts and limitations. Rather than a simple choice between the selfless choice and the selfish choice, we need to all be selfless in our various roles and duties.

The diverse gifts given to God's people is a good thing that should never be undermined by zealous vision casting that implies there are different classes of Christians.

## Content with the circumstances of your calling

The last perspective on the realities of life that God gives us in 1 Corinthians 7 is that of contentment. But in this passage contentment is not merely the virtue of patience that you must summon up to help you cope with difficult circumstances, fuelled by deep satisfaction in the goodness of God and the hope of heaven. Here the logic is not, "Oh well, never mind, at least God loves you and you're going to heaven." In this passage, contentment rests on our awareness of our calling:

> Nevertheless, each person should live as a believer in whatever situation the Lord has assigned to them, just as God has called them. This is the rule I lay down in all the churches. Was a man already circumcised when he was called? He should not become uncircumcised. Was a man uncircumcised when he was called? He should not be circumcised. Circumcision is nothing and uncircumcision is nothing. Keeping God's commands is what counts. Each person should remain in the situation they were in when God called them.
>
> Were you a slave when you were called? Don't let it trouble you—although if you can gain your freedom,

   THE GOOD LIFE IN THE LAST DAYS

do so. For the one who was a slave when called to faith in the Lord is the Lord's freed person; similarly, the one who was free when called is Christ's slave. You were bought at a price; do not become slaves of human beings. Brothers and sisters, each person, as responsible to God, should remain in the situation they were in when God called them. (1 Cor 7:17-24)

Verse 17 tells you that wherever you were *when you were called by God* is now the place *where you are called to serve God*. So verses 18 and 19 encourage you that you don't have to change the circumstances of your life in order to serve God meaningfully, you are not enslaved by your circumstances. So you can be joyfully content—more, genuinely satisfied—in whatever situation you find yourself in. Right here, right now can be your holy calling: this is the life you have been given, so keep God's commands where you are. This truth is not intended to restrict us, after all verse 21 counsels the slave "if you can gain your freedom, do so". Elsewhere in the passage he permits the single person to marry if they so choose. This teaching is not meant to encourage apathy or justify oppressive social structures, but to give freedom to serve God wherever you are.

In his book *Status Anxiety*, Alain de Botton observes that discontentment is a particular challenge that we face in the modern Western World, because of the possibility of social mobility. Due to a "practical belief in the innate equality of all humans and the unlimited power of anyone to achieve anything",[104] we are unable to be content with our current

104  Alain de Botton, *Status Anxiety,* Penguin, London, 2005, p. 47.

status in life.[105] There's probably some truth to that, don't you think? But discontentment is not unique to the modern world. Calvin also addresses it well:

> The Lord enjoins every one of us, in all the actions of life, to have respect to our own calling. He knows the boiling restlessness of the human mind, the fickleness with which it is borne hither and thither, its eagerness to hold opposites at one time in its grasp, its ambition. Therefore, lest all things should be thrown into confusion by our folly and rashness, he has assigned distinct duties to each in the different modes of life… Every man's mode of life, therefore, is a kind of station assigned him by the Lord, that he may not be always driven about at random.[106]

Are you ruled by your circumstances? Driven to bitterness or despair because they are not what you hoped they would be? Or proud and joyful because things are going well? We are slaves of Christ wherever we are, we are freed in Christ wherever we are. We were bought by his blood, and so our lives now belong to him (vv. 22-23). Others can be awful to us and our life circumstances can be horrible—or just annoying: the boss, the church elders, the in-laws, the local council, the weather, the aching knees… But how do you respond to such things, in Christ? Do you give in to a grumbling and resentful spirit? In so doing you are slowly being enslaved by your circumstances. The great truth of contentment in our calling is to realize: this is it. Our current circumstances are not an

---

105    de Botton, *Status Anxiety,* pp. 45-63.
106    Calvin, *Institutes,* book III, chapter 10, section 6.

                          THE GOOD LIFE IN THE LAST DAYS

interference in our lives. This is our calling right now. Serve God contentedly in the midst of it.

Such an outlook goes against all sorts of received wisdom. For example, there is an old proverb that says, "A wife halves or doubles a husband's ministry." This proverb is doubtless used to encourage a woman in the powerful ways her support can assist in her husband's ministry of the word. In the right context it might even be a helpful reminder that her discouraging words can have a massive impact too. But it is also prone to extremely unhelpful misunderstanding and misapplication. How easily a wife could feel crushed by the burden that her natural limitations, beyond her control, are 'halving' her husband's ministry.

Another potential problem with focusing on how a woman might halve or double her husband's ministry is that her significance becomes tied to the degree in which she helps or hinders her husband's role or ministry, rather than focusing on her own unique set of gifts and opportunities, some of which might extend beyond her husband's ministry. It obscures the fact that she shares in her husband's ministry, it is hers as well as his. And it also ignores the fact that loving his wife is part of the husband's ministry. She is not merely a human resource to double his ministry, but an inseparable part of his life and ministry—they are one flesh, after all. In that sense, his wife cannot double or halve his ministry: she *is* part of his ministry.[107] Michael Jensen reflects on this theme as it is found in the character of the would-be Christian missionary St. John Rivers from the novel *Jane Eyre*:

107 And indeed he is part of *her* ministry, and by loving her supports her in the ministries she is engaged in that extend beyond him.

A young man, full of zeal for the Lord, will be told to choose a wife who will double his ministry, and not halve it. Young wives are told this too. There are husbands who will sacrifice the mental health and well-being of their partners on the altar of their ministry ambitions. There are those of us who will cling to the ministry long past the stage when it is obvious that we should choose a calling that puts less stress on a particular family. There are children who report being shunted aside by parents in favour of the higher needs of the ministry, for 'the sake of the gospel'.

A woman known to me said that her first, violently abusive husband used the very same rhetoric on her.

St. John Rivers' idealism is not unfamiliar. And the wreckage he leaves around him isn't unfamiliar either.

What is spiritually wrong with St. John Rivers is that he doesn't understand the very Gospel he claims to preach. He doesn't understand that that Gospel is not a project, or a cause, to which all, including people, must be sacrificed. It is rather, a message which is essentially about love. You cannot demand Jane Eyre marry you and submit herself to your holy work, because it isn't loving. You can't act like a jerk at home, and justify it because you have an important part to play in God's plan for the world.

There might be deities you can serve in that way, but Jesus of Nazareth is not one of them.[108]

---

108  Michael Jensen, 'Jane Eyre and St John Rivers, and the Ministry Marriage', *The Gospel Coalition Australia,* 5 December 2015 (viewed 1 November 2017): https://australia.thegospelcoalition.org/article/jane-eyre-and-st-john-rivers-and-the-ministry-marriage

Be content with your circumstances, knowing that in the first place you are called to serve Christ where you are. Paul uses this principle to warn married people against abandoning their marriage in pursuit of the ideal of a more spiritual life and he also uses it to encourage single people to consider the possibility of remaining single. One of the easiest forms of ethical decision-making is to remain as you already are.

## It's complicated and that's biblical

You might have picked up this book feeling that the challenges of living life and sacrificing for Christ were complicated and hoping for some simple answers to guide you. You might have even felt guilty about the ways that your life is complicated and wondered if this book would rebuke you for not really living in the light of eternity. But the purpose of this chapter is to show that 'it's complicated' is actually biblical. It's not just the resigned shrug of ordinary people who can't figure it out, or won't face the way things ought to be. God himself, as he speaks to us in his word, acknowledges and affirms the diversity and limitations of our experience and urges us to serve him in and through these things rather than by somehow overruling them.

So how do we figure out when to sacrifice more? Or make a radical decision for Christ? How do we justify a more conservative path? That's what we will look at in the final chapters.

**7**

# PUTTING IT INTO PRACTICE: DECISION-MAKING UNDER THE WORD OF GOD

I'm a keen 'aggressive inline skater': I like to do tricks on rollerblades. I started roller-skating when I was 10 years old, started inline skating when I was 12 years old and stopped after a serious knee injury when I was 15. A few years ago when the kids wanted skates for Christmas, I bought myself a pair as well and have really enjoyed getting back into it again. Now, exactly how many hours can I justify spending at the skate park especially given that the time is short and the gospel needs to be preached? Six hours a week? Four hours? What if I justify it by saying that this is how I keep my body in good shape to serve the Lord? Does that help? What if I wear a Christian University Union t-shirt and try to chat to the scooter kids about Jesus? How much money should I spend on a new pair of inline skates? Should I take up a cheaper hobby like jogging so that I can give more to my church?

It's a silly example on one level, but on another level these are exactly the kinds of decisions we have to make all the time. They are decisions that can tie us in knots. Some of us give up hobbies we love altogether because we cannot see how we can continue them in good conscience. Some of us continue with our hobby, but in a discreet and slightly embarrassed manner: when the topic comes up at church we might quickly shift the conversation to more 'spiritual' matters. Still others among us have no qualms at all about our hobbies but only because we are not really concerned about how to live well in these last days at all.

The difficulties we experience with decisions regarding hobbies also arise in almost every other area of our Christian lives: how many hours should I devote to church ministry? How much money should I give to charity? Can I justify not inviting international students to join our family Christmas lunch? What about when these decisions come at the expense of my family and me? Is it good to miss my child's school play because I am on the parish Nomination Committee? Is it better to structure my budget to be gospel generous in a way that rules out interstate holidays? When should inconvenience or distress for my family be a reason for saying 'no' to an opportunity to practice hospitality?

In this book's final two chapters I want to show from 1 Corinthians 7 that the biblical answer is that there is no one answer to these questions. Instead, under the word of God we should think things through carefully and then… do what we want.

    THE GOOD LIFE IN THE LAST DAYS

## Under the word of God

The first thing is that we must make all our decisions and weigh all our options under the word of God. This is a simple outworking of the principles we explored in chapter 1: God comes before, above, at the centre and as the ultimate end of our lives. Because the ordinary way that God speaks with his people is in Scripture, we need to treat Scripture with the same reverence, trust and obedience that we accord to God. In *Guidance and the Voice of God,* Phillip Jensen and Tony Payne give a big-picture summary of how God guides his people. They show that "God is leading his people to… heaven, to be submitted finally and completely to Christ, and to be conformed to his image. God has set the destination and, in his great power and love, makes sure we get there. Along the way, he has good works for us to walk in and calls us to response to his leading."[109] They then give "five propositions about how God guides":

1. God, in his sovereignty, uses everything to guide us 'behind the scenes'.
2. In many and varied ways, God *can* speak to his people, and guide them with their conscious cooperation.
3. In these last days, God has spoken to us by his Son.
4. God speaks to us today by his Son through his Spirit in the Scriptures.
5. Apart from his Spirit working through Scripture, God does not promise to use any other means to guide us, nor should we expect him to.[110]

---

109  Phillip Jensen and Tony Payne, *Guidance and the Voice of God,* Matthias Media, Sydney, 1997, p. 71.

110  Jensen and Payne, *Guidance and the Voice of God,* pp. 76-7.

Where this is clear, figuring out *what* to do is easy, even if trusting God and obeying him can be very difficult. No decision which disbelieves and disobeys God's good word is the right decision. For example, if a Christian is exclusively same-sex attracted it can be a great challenge to trust God and resolve to live a single life. It can be a very painful sacrifice to give up the possibility of sexual intimacy for the sake of godliness. But for the Christian, this is both the right thing to do and the best thing to do.[111]

But living according to God's word is more than just figuring out all the explicit commands.

## God's word and wisdom

God's purpose for his people is not simply that we be submissive and obedient but that we become wise decision makers (Rom 12:2; Phil 1:9-10). As we understand more about who God is, and his plans for the world, we become wise.[112] Wisdom also captures all the things discussed in chapter 2: loving people (and treating things) as they are, where they are, when they are; while knowing who we are, where we are and when we are. We might wish it was all a matter of obeying the rules, following the steps in the manual, plugging data into a spread sheet and getting the right result, but our heavenly Father has something more rich and glorious in view. Oliver O'Donovan describes the Christian life this way:

111    See Ed Shaw, *The Plausibility Problem* (IVP, London, 2015) for a wonderful exploration of what it is like to make this decision.
112    Goldsworthy, 'Gospel and Wisdom'. See also Schrage, *The Ethics of the New Testament,* pp. 197-8.

In Christ, man was able for the first time to assume his proper place with [the world], the place of dominion which God assigned to Adam. Thus Christian freedom, given by the Holy Spirit, allows man to make moral responses creatively… As a moral agent, he is involved in deciding what a situation is and [what a situation] demands in the light of the moral order. As a moral agent in history he has to interpret *new* situations, plumbing their meanings and declaring them by his decisions.[113]

Because of this we need to continually hear the word of God and be shaped and guided by it so we interpret things rightly. But we also need to be alert to the created world itself because wisdom recognizes that the Creator made his creation with order and purposes that we can recognize, when guided by his word: "Wisdom is [the] name for that package of experience, discernment and knowledgeable love of God that enables a good life".[114] God's word interprets his world to us and sends us out into it with open eyes and ears. Without such wisdom we are unable to face the challenge of decision-making.

In doing this we not only make wise choices but we become *wise people*. And this godly character actually further helps us in the challenges of decision-making.

113    O'Donovan, *Resurrection and Moral Order,* p. 24.
114    Cameron, *Joined-Up Life,* p. 153. See also his excellent epilogue 'Dilemmas and Discernment', pp. 312-17.

## God's word and Christian character

I like lasagne and horror movies. When I was growing up I was a cat person but since we got our dog, Sophie, I've swapped sides. I am an ENTJ on the Myers-Briggs Type Indicator and a Di in the DiSC behaviour assessment tool. But when we talk about 'character', we are talking about something more than 'personality'. Our character is the settled pattern of our thoughts, feeling and actions.[115] This character is formed in us by God the Holy Spirit. He does not simply lead us through a series of discreet moral decisions but grows fruit within us: "love, joy, peace, forbearance, kindness, goodness, faithfulness, gentleness and self-control" (Gal 5:22-23). This process is also described as us having "Christ… formed in [us]" (Gal 4:19), being "renewed in knowledge in the image of [our] Creator" (Col 3:10) and even "participat[ing] in the divine nature" (2 Pet 1:4). As we make individual decisions our character is formed and this character in turn influences the decisions we make in the future.

Our Christian character is the outworking of our identity in Christ. We should not look at ourselves "from a worldly point of view" (2 Cor 5:16) and focus on our family background, social status and physical appearance. Instead we need to know who we are in Christ: "if anyone is in Christ, the new creation has come: The old has gone, the new is here!" (v. 17). And, knowing who we are, we need to live in light of our new identity. As Paul writes:

---

**115**　Hill, *The How and Why of Love*, pp. 36-40; O'Donovan, *Resurrection and Moral Order*, pp. 204-18.

For you were once darkness, but now you are light in the Lord. Live as children of light (for the fruit of the light consists in all goodness, righteousness and truth) and find out what pleases the Lord. Have nothing to do with the fruitless deeds of darkness, but rather expose them. It is shameful even to mention what the disobedient do in secret. But everything exposed by the light becomes visible—and everything that is illuminated becomes a light. (Eph 5:8-13)

Our identity brings with it a story too.[116] We are actors in God's great salvation history. We are his precious creatures created in his image to rule the world, but shamefully we responded in outrageous rebellion against him, to our misery and condemnation. But because of God's great love for us he has promised to save the fallen human race and in the fullness of time sent his Son to live, die and rise as the saviour king. We are now in the last days, preaching the gospel of his salvation to the ends of the earth and waiting for him to return from heaven, to judge and to save. Our final hope is to glorify God and enjoy his gloriously new and perfect creation for ever and ever. This is the big story that our little stories fit into. And knowing this big story helps us make sense of how to think and feel and act. As John describes:

See what great love the Father has lavished on us, that we should be called children of God! And that is what

---

116 Stanley Hauerwas, 'A Retrospective Assessment of an "Ethics of Character": The Development of Hauerwas's Theological Project (1985, 2001)' in *The Hauerwas Reader,* pp. 74-89.

we are! The reason the world does not know us is that it did not know him. Dear friends, now we are children of God, and what we will be has not yet been made known. But we know that when Christ appears, we shall be like him, for we shall see him as he is. All who have this hope in him purify themselves, just as he is pure. (1 John 3:1-3)

How does all of this help us in the process of making the tricky decisions of life, especially when it comes to figuring out the details of how to live in the light of the second coming of Christ? *In the first place, understanding the importance of character shaped and moulded by God's word takes the pressure off figuring everything out.* As we grow in Christian character we will increasingly want to do the godly thing, we will begin to love what God loves and hate what he hates, and we will begin to play the part God has assigned to us in his larger story.

*In the second place, we need a godly character to be able to do the right thing in the moment.* When we encounter a tough decision which requires us to suffer for the name of Christ, it is in one sense 'already too late' to start thinking about what we should do. At the point of temptation we will be drawing on the convictions and character that have already been formed in us.

*In the third place, the idea of character gives us the reflective tool: 'What kind of person will this make me?'* This question is a blunt instrument in many ways. Character is not easily read off the surface of any one choice. If talk about character is the primary way of thinking about decisions, it can end up masking pre-existing assumptions and prejudices, in the way

          THE GOOD LIFE IN THE LAST DAYS

that asking 'What Would Jesus Do?' is often simply 'What would I do when I imagine what Jesus would do?' But as a thought experiment it can be a powerful way to gain a larger perspective on my actions. I might refuse a particular kind of honour or luxury that is offered to me because 'I don't want to be the kind of guy who does things for worldly gain'. In such cases the offer was not itself evil but accepting it might form part of a whole character of life that might become evil.

We must make decisions with godly wisdom and character, under the word of God. All this is at work in 1 Corinthians 7. Paul doesn't tell his readers exactly what to do with black-and-white rules nor does he leave it completely up in the air. Instead he writes a long chapter of instruction and exhortation to inform their decision-making, pointing out:

- the importance of moral purity (vv. 1-16)
- the value of accepting your circumstances and serving God wherever you are (vv. 17-24)
- the reality that the time is short (vv. 29-31)
- the practical benefits of singleness (vv. 25-28, 32-35 and 39-40).[117]

As we prayerfully receive these things and take them to heart we will be properly equipped to make decisions about marriage and singleness and many other things besides. Christian freedom must always be exercised under the word of God.

Because God is forming our whole lives by his word we don't need step-by-step instruction, nor do we need to be in

---

117   And chapter 7 is a part of the whole letter of 1 Corinthians which indirectly informs and enriches how we read and apply it.

a constant state of intense decision-making. Instead we will find that there tend to be seasons of reflection followed by seasons of living it out.

## Seasons of thinking

We don't need to be in a constant state of crisis and re-evaluation, constantly second-guessing what is the best configuration of our lives. This kind of approach would be traumatic and ineffective for the cause of Christ and for loving others. It is right to settle down and serve Christ in the situation we are already in (1 Cor 7:17-24). As finite creatures we cannot mentally or emotionally maintain a vivid and immediate awareness of the blinding glory of God, the joy of eternal life and the horror of eternal judgement. Those who try to constantly contemplate eternal realities with such intensity tend to be hindered rather than helped in godly usefulness. As Richard Baxter wisely observes:

> The intending of God's glory or our spiritual good, cannot be distinctly and sensibly re-acted in every particular pleasure we take, or bit we eat, or thing we use: but a sincere Habitual Intention well laid at first in the Heart, will serve to the right use of many particular Means.[118]

However, there will be times when we need to stop, reflect and make decisions afresh. There is no one perfect pattern for the Christian life, no single playbook or Excel spreadsheet that we can figure out and then just maintain until Christ

118  Richard Baxter quoted in Rigney, *The Things of Earth*, p. 123.

returns. Things can change in small and big ways. This is part of the reason we need to keep hearing and meditating on God's word. Not only do we discover more about God's glory and goodness, his word will continue to speak to us as we experience change in our lives. The word of God about fathers and sons in Ephesians 6:1-4 has one application to a young man in youth group, learning how to respect his dad; another to the same man as he has kids of his own; and still another as he figures out how to care for his father in old age. The same biblical warning against envy, might become a very urgent word if this is the current temptation threatening me. A fresh reading of the Great Commission can be the final catalyst in a bold new move to join a church plant core team.

As Hebrews 3 wonderfully applies Psalm 95: *today* we need to hear his voice and not harden our hearts, we need to encourage one another *daily* not to be hardened by sin's deceitfulness. Through personal quiet times, informal 'one another' ministry and public Bible teaching we are guided by our loving Father by his living word, applied by the Holy Spirit to our minds and hearts.

There will be particular times that call for sustained reflection and fresh decision-making. Often these new seasons are thrust upon us by circumstances: in 1 Corinthians 7:15 it is being abandoned by one's spouse, in verse 21 it is a slave getting the option to gain their freedom and in verse 39 it is becoming a widow. In each of these cases there comes a new season, with new decisions and new factors to consider: how to serve Christ in the last days in this new set of circumstances? Sometimes the circumstances that provoke a change might be less concrete and dramatic: a particular sermon or Bible verse might illuminate our minds and prick our consciences in such a way that we feel stirred to a new kind of action. Or the kids might grow up and go to school, or our enthusiasm and interests shift in subtle ways. For various reasons we reach a point where a new assessment of how to live for Christ is needed.

Wise preaching will recognize these realities. We need preaching that will do the kinds of things that Paul does in 1 Corinthians 7, to fully inform our minds and hearts and even provoke us to consider decisions we haven't entertained. Many years ago I was speaking to some missionaries working with university students in Paris. At that time there was not a culture of public preaching in French student ministry. They observed that it was harder to call Christian university students to consider full-time Christian ministry without preaching, the way they themselves had experienced back in Australia. Preaching can give the big picture of God's purposes, engage the emotions and so challenge the congregation in ways that it is harder to do in the context of inductive Bible study and personal mentoring.[119]

But wise preaching will also recognize that there are seasons of thinking. Every single congregation member won't have a life-changing crisis every single time they hear a sermon. Skilful preaching will bring sweeping challenges while also leaving space for individual Christians to respond in different ways, possibly by realizing that their response to God's word is to stay their course. Those who preach should weigh their words and rhetoric carefully. They must not

119   Of course, 1 Corinthians is not a sermon but a letter. In some ways the written word, whether in letters or books, also has a particular kind of impact.

over-reach in an effort to give their preaching that extra 'oomph'. The teaching might sound more 'challenging' and stir up some to great things, but in the process it might also trample on Christian freedom and crush fellow believers. Kevin DeYoung and Greg Gilbert give great advice to preachers in the brilliant epilogue of *What is the Mission of the Church?*

> Go big on the big principles and not as big on the specific application… Go big and crazy with the broad principles—no holds barred, no caveats. But once you start talking specifics—in your sermons, in counselling, in discipleship—we ought to be a little more nuanced and careful…
>
> Whatever gets in the way of… radical allegiance [to Jesus] is trouble, be it family, money, job, status, pleasure, rule keeping, whatever. So don't be afraid to tell people that Jesus needs to come before all these things. But be careful not to overspecify what this looks like…
>
> One of the most important jobs of a pastor is to help people feel guilty when they are guilty and help people feel at peace when they are not guilty. Oftentimes, young pastors, especially passionate ones, are eager for their people to feel guilty about most everything. It's one of the ways we know we are getting through to people.[120]

Likewise, as we listen to preaching we need to find a way to distance ourselves from particular challenges that may not

---

120  DeYoung and Gilbert, *Mission of the Church,* pp. 257-60.

be directly relevant to us in the moment. We need to guard against personalizing every single sermon application without discernment, while also remaining attentive and open to the word. And this is even more important where the preacher might be guilty of over-reach and be urging on our consciences things that God's word does not require of us. Listening to imperfect, human teachers always requires a healthy mix of humility and discernment (1 Thess 5:19-22).

So then, let's say that you are sitting under the word of God and meditating on it regularly in repentance and faith. Over time God has been making you more and more wise and discerning; he has formed a godly character in you, not in sinless perfection, but still in genuine spiritual maturity. Now let's say that you have reached another season of change where you need to make a big life decision. How do you proceed?

**8**

# PUTTING IT INTO PRACTICE: DECISION-MAKING WITH CHRISTIAN FREEDOM

At the end of a long argument in 1 Corinthians 7 Paul reaches a surprising conclusion:

> If anyone is worried that he might not be acting honourably toward the virgin he is engaged to, and if his passions are too strong and he feels he ought to marry, *he should do as he wants.* He is not sinning. They should get married. *But the man who has settled the matter in his own mind, who is under no compulsion but has control over his own will, and who has made up his mind* not to marry the virgin—this man also does the right thing. So then, he who marries the virgin does right, but he who does not marry her does better. (vv. 36-38)

"He should do as he wants"! It almost sounds wrong, doesn't it? Is the Christian moral path ever "Do what you want to?"

Clearly in this case, it is. And if his answer is surprising to us then perhaps we need to take a bit more time to properly understand Christian freedom.

## Understanding Christian freedom

In 1 Corinthians 7 we find a sustained affirmation of Christian freedom to choose. As Andrew Cameron says, "Paul practically does somersaults to convince his readers that *there's such a thing as two right answers*":[121]

- "I say this as a concession, not as a command." (v. 6)
- "I have no command from the Lord, but I give a judgement as one who by the Lord's mercy is trustworthy… But if you do marry, you have not sinned; and if a virgin marries, she has not sinned." (vv. 25, 28)
- "I am saying this for your own good, not to restrict you, but that you may live in a right way in undivided devotion to the Lord." (v. 35)
- "A woman is bound to her husband as long as he lives. But if her husband dies, she is free to marry anyone she wishes, but he must belong to the Lord." (v. 39)

Christians are free in many ways. *We are free from the world* (Gal 1:4), *sin* (Rom 8:1-4, Titus 2:14), *death, the wrath of God, the devil and the law of the Sinai covenant* (Gal 3:13-14 and Heb 2:14-17). Christians are no longer controlled and constrained by the evil forces that shame us and shrink us. We are no longer condemned to face death and eternal judgement—by the grace of God in the cross of Christ we are set free.

121  Cameron, *Joined-Up Life,* p. 236.

But the Christian gospel is not just about what we are freed *from*, as if we get saved from Hell to then do whatever we please. Now, by the power of his Spirit *we are free to live lives that are pleasing to him in line with who we were created and redeemed to be* (John 8:34-36; Gal 5:1, 13). In coming to Christ we become more ourselves than we ever were before. When you live according to the sinful nature, even as you consciously make your own decisions, your mind is darkened by sin so that you are unable to consistently make decisions according to God's truth—you are a slave to your own desires and thoughts. But in Christ we are free to think, desire and act truly and rightly.

More still, *we are actually free in a greater way than the people of Israel or even Adam and Eve in Eden: for we are now sons of God in Christ Jesus,*[122] *with the Spirit of Sonship dwelling in us* (Gal 3:26-4:7). We have a new intimacy of relationship with God, which brings with it a new kind of privilege.

Now that we are free from sin and death and free to live for God as sons, we are also *free to choose to live lives that please him by choosing among many good possibilities.* We enjoy a generous freedom as sons and daughters in the kingdom of God.[123]

---

**122**   I have chosen to write only "sons of God" rather than "sons and daughters of God" to capture the New Testament emphasis that this sonship is grounded in Jesus' sonship and enjoys the same notions of being heirs of God.

**123**   All of this points out that freedom is more than just having as many options available to us as possible. Without understanding our nature and purpose, boundless freedom is a very sad and oddly enslaving thing. See O'Donovan, *Resurrection and Moral Order,* pp. 107-9.

## The problem with legalism

This is why the various things we call 'legalism' are great enemies of the gospel: for each kind of 'legalism' undermines the freedom the gospel gives us. One kind of legalism seeks *to cooperate with God to earn our righteousness by obedience.* This kind of legalism denies the full and perfect salvation won for us in Christ: "If righteousness could be gained through the law, Christ died for nothing!" (Gal 2:21).

A second kind of legalism is *the legalistic attitude of proud self-justification and mean-spirited judgementalism,* which undermines the humble, merciful spirit we are called to: "I desire mercy not sacrifice" (Hos 6:6, quoted by Jesus in Matt 9:13 and 12:7).

A third kind of legalism undermines the Christian freedom to choose between many good possible things. This kind of legalism *adds to God's word with new rules and unbiblical pedantry.* In adding to God's word it ends up removing the many godly options that God does in fact give us and tends to undermine the goodness of the created world itself: "deceiving spirits and things taught by demons… forbid people to marry and order them to abstain from certain foods, which God created to be received with thanksgiving" (1 Tim 4:1, 3). It might seem like a small thing, to worry about what people can choose to eat or drink or wear, but Calvin explains the ultimate outcome of this kind of legalism. He writes that many think it is a minor thing to worry about Christian freedom related to food or clothes or holy days. But although these things *seem* like "frivolous trifles" they are actually "of more importance than is commonly supposed". Because once your conscience starts doubting whether something is really good or not, you get "entangled in a net" and enter a "labyrinth from which it is afterwards most difficult to escape." To use a modern example, once you start doubting whether it is right for Christians to enjoy the luxury of going to a premium cinema, you start asking questions about the regular cinema, or even renting a film off iTunes, until eventually you discover you feel uneasy about watching films altogether—and start having qualms about board games![124] The end result of adding rules and laws over and above the word of God is that we end up denying the goodness of God's created world.

## Freedom from human teachings and rules

The apostles wrote a lot about Christian freedom as they guided churches through different attitudes to food sacrificed to pagan idols, Jewish food laws and holy days. They strongly affirmed that Jewish food laws are not morally binding on Christians:

> I am convinced, being fully persuaded in the Lord Jesus, that nothing is unclean in itself… All food is clean… (Rom 14:14, 20b)

> Food does not bring us near to God; we are no worse if we do not eat, and no better if we do… Eat anything sold in the meat market without raising questions of conscience, for, "The earth is the Lord's, and everything in it". (1 Cor 8:8, 10:25-26)

124  Calvin, *Institutes,* book III, chapter 19, section 7.

Because of this, we must not condemn other Christians on such matters for they are not answerable to us, but personally answerable to the Lord:

> The one who eats everything must not treat with contempt the one who does not, and the one who does not eat everything must not judge the one who does, for God has accepted them. Who are you to judge someone else's servant? To their own master, servants stand or fall. And they will stand, for the Lord is able to make them stand…
>
> For none of us lives for ourselves alone, and none of us dies for ourselves alone. If we live, we live for the Lord; and if we die, we die for the Lord. So, whether we live or die, we belong to the Lord. For this very reason, Christ died and returned to life so that he might be the Lord of both the dead and the living…
>
> You, then, why do you judge your brother or sister? Or why do you treat them with contempt? For we will all stand before God's judgement seat…
>
> Therefore let us stop passing judgement on one another. (Rom 14:3-4, 7-10, 13a)

In the 16th and 17th centuries, the Reformers and the Puritans picked up this theme of Christian freedom. They were reacting to the Roman Catholic Church (and in some cases, the Church of England), which had added many laws for the Christian life and many rituals to the practice of Christian Sunday gatherings which went well beyond the word of God. The Westminster Confession of Faith has a whole chapter on 'Christian Liberty' where it says:



THE GOOD LIFE IN THE LAST DAYS

God alone is Lord of the conscience, and has left it free from the doctrines and commandments of men, which are, in any thing, contrary to His Word; or beside it, in matters of faith, or worship.[125]

In other words, God is the only one who can tell us what to believe about him and God is the only one who can tell us how to serve him. We are free from human teachings and rules that contradict or add to God's word; no government or bishop has a right to add to or overturn God's word and expect believers to obey their authority. The Confession goes on to say:

To believe such doctrines, or to obey such commands… is to betray true liberty of conscience: and the requiring of an implicit faith, and an absolute and blind obedience, is to destroy liberty of conscience, and reason also.

Three important implications flow from this teaching. We will look at two of these here and a third under 'The Abuse of Freedom' below. *Firstly, our individual responsibility before God is so important and the pangs of conscience so easily deadened, that a believer should act in line with their conscience even if it is misguided* (Rom 14:14, 23; 1 Cor 8:7). In the Bible conscience is not some source of moral knowledge. It's not as if there are some religious and moral things that can't be known in any other way, so we have to turn to an intuition of conscience to know what is right. Rather, in the Bible our

---

125 'Of Christian Liberty, and Liberty of Conscience', *The Westminster Confession of Faith,* Center for Reformed Theology and Apologetics (viewed 31 October 2017): www.reformed.org/documents/wcf_with_proofs/. See also Robert Letham, *The Westminster Assembly: Reading its Theology in Historical Context,* P&R, Phillipsburg, 2001, p. 299.

conscience is our self-awareness, particularly as it relates to having done the right thing or the wrong thing. It is not so much a source of moral guidance as it is an awareness of guilt.[126] God urges us to act in line with our conscience, even if it might be weak and misguided. To go against our current self-awareness is to act in bad faith and runs the risk of hardening our hearts. Over time our conscience might grow stronger and better informed, but we must act in line with where we are currently.

The second implication, not explicitly taught in Scripture, is that a wise church leadership or civil government will consider where and how to allow freedom on points of disagreement regarding religion and morals. To leave room for individual responsibility and the ultimate lordship of God, it is good and right to restrain the reach of human authorities, even if they are not adding to God's word but only seeking to enforce it. This is where a second use of the term 'liberty of conscience' comes about: to mean the social freedom for all citizens to follow their personal convictions about religion and morality, even if the convictions are not biblical. This is not the biblical meaning of the term but a reasonable consequence of it.

Freedom to choose between many different good things doesn't contradict the other types of freedom: we are free from sin to serve God, we are not free to sin (Rom 6:15; Gal 5:13; 1 Pet 2:16; Jude 4). Rather, this freedom is exclusively in those matters of choosing between different possible good options.

---

126 Schrage, *The Ethics of the New Testament,* p. 195.

   THE GOOD LIFE IN THE LAST DAYS

## Freedom in matters of good judgement and triviality

In *Guidance and the Voice of God* Phillip Jensen and Tony Payne give a series of categories that help us in understanding our freedom as Christians. Firstly, we should consider 'matters of righteousness', secondly, we should also consider 'matters of good judgement' and then lastly we should recognize that there remain many things that are 'matters of triviality'.[127] The categories aren't completely distinct[128] but they definitely help us get clear on the areas where Christians are free.

*We are obviously free in 'matters of triviality'.* These are matters where the choice is neither clearly about right and wrong, nor even 'good' or 'better'. As Jensen and Payne write, "Wisdom will… tell us that some decisions are of such little consequence, that they are not worth wasting time and energy on… the wise person will see that it can be a mistake to invest too much importance in decisions that really are trivial".[129] Getting perspective on what things aren't of crucial importance is extremely liberating. However, the idea of 'matters of triviality' can become distorted so that we begin

---

**127**    Jensen and Payne, *Guidance and the Voice of God,* p. 105.

**128**    As Jensen and Payne acknowledge: We mustn't think that wisdom is some entirely optional, slightly grey area for the spiritually mature. In the Bible, it is righteous to be wise, and the truly wise are righteous (see for example the introduction to the book of Proverbs). Many particular 'wise' things are also required of God's people, rather than optional: for example laziness and drunkenness are only explicitly condemned in the Old Testament in the wisdom literature. Wisdom also informs how to live the righteous life, helping us know the godly decision in any particular context: when to be firm and when to be flexible, for example (*Guidance and the Voice of God*, p. 105).

**129**    Jensen and Payne, *Guidance and the Voice of God,* p. 111. The Stoic Philosophers before the time of Jesus called these things 'adiaphora': morally indistinguishable things.

to think that some things are trivial *in and of themselves*. Take circumcision, for example. In 1 Corinthians 7:19 Paul writes, "Circumcision is nothing and uncircumcision is nothing. Keeping God's commands is what counts." Clearly then, circumcision is a 'matter of triviality'. But this doesn't mean that circumcision is absolutely trivial, for in Romans the very same apostle writes, "What advantage, then, is there in being a Jew, or what value is there in circumcision? Much in every way!" (Rom 3:1-2a). For circumcision is a precious social, cultural and God-given sign; it is not absolutely trivial.[130]

To be clearer then, we need to say that 'matters of triviality' are 'matters of *relative* triviality, so far as the godly life is concerned'. For nothing is entirely indifferent in God's good creation. The risk of misunderstanding when we talk about 'matters of triviality' is that we can convey 'This thing doesn't matter' at all'. So if you like it, care about it, appreciate it, spend time on it, you are necessarily wasteful, foolish, trivial, trifling, sinful.

*We are also free in some 'matters of good judgement'.* The kind of 'good judgement' that is distinct from 'righteousness' is about judging between multiple options, where one may be wiser or in some way better than the other. This is what we find in 1 Corinthians 7: both marriage and singleness are "good", but Paul's wisdom advises that singleness is even "better" than marriage. Such situations are rarely simple because given the limitation, uniqueness and circumstances of a particular person (as we explored in chapter 6), for them

---

130 And, as Paul discusses in Galatians 2:1-10, in some circumstances, getting circumcised would be a *bad* thing!

  THE GOOD LIFE IN THE LAST DAYS

the "good" option might actually be better than the generally "better" option. True wisdom takes into account the full picture, including all the peculiarities of my particular situation. In fact, it is often impossible to make a full assessment of all the factors so that we can come up with a single, undeniable 'wisest possible choice'. True wisdom recognizes the reality of the limitations of human wisdom.

In my own experience, in the everyday 'folk ethics' that grows up around those of us serious to serve Christ with wisdom and discernment, "matters of good judgement" can easily take on the force of a moral obligation. I know that I and other earnest Christians I have known and ministered to have felt bound to choose the 'wisest possible option'. This wisest option is often the kind of thing that has become 'received wisdom' in our particular Christian community, or family upbringing. But this is not the case, as Paul stresses throughout 1 Corinthians 7. In cases where there are practical benefits and reasons to favour one thing over another, we are not bound to always choose the "better" thing in some abstract sense. True wisdom recognizes the factors to take into account include our personal preferences and desires. If we have thought it through and made up our mind on the matter in wisdom and godliness, we are free to act as we see fit in such circumstances (vv. 36-38). 'Better' options don't have the same moral demand on us that 'moral' actions do. Joe Rigney says, "Giving up a luxury car for the sake of Christ is different from giving up a stolen car".[131] Christians are free in Christ not only to choose between matters of equal importance (or unimportance) but free to choose differently

131 Rigney, *The Things of Earth,* p. 179.

from one another. We may freely choose something that someone else would regard as less wise, less commendable, or less strategic. Wisdom for us means choosing that which, in light of everything (including our personal preferences and desires), makes most sense of what is in front of us. The "better" option is commendable—and Paul spends a lot of time commending it throughout 1 Corinthians 7—but he is also careful not to mandate this choice.

## Freedom to do what you want to do

The way God's word directs our choices isn't purely intellectual. Love for God and neighbour shapes our whole character with virtues that fuel and direct our desires. Our character is slowly formed in us as we hear God's word, and repent, believe and obey by the power of God's Holy Spirit in community with our fellow believers.[132] Many of the things we do are not the result of isolated, deliberate rational reflection, but the natural expression of who we are and what we value. Because we have not yet been made perfect, however, we will also experience the conflict between the desires of the flesh and the desires of the Spirit pulling in two different directions (Gal 5:16-17). Nevertheless, insofar as we are following the desires formed in us by the Spirit, we will discover more and more that we choose what is good not simply because we *ought to*, but because we *want to*. Far from being a fickle, trivial, emotional thing, desire is part of what makes a choice truly personal and sincere.

The apostle Paul preserves Christian freedom throughout

132 Cameron, *Joined-Up Life,* pp. 36-9, 49-55, 120-7.

 THE GOOD LIFE IN THE LAST DAYS

1 Corinthians 7, and underlines it emphatically in verse 36 and 37:

> If anyone is worried that he might not be acting honourably toward the virgin he is engaged to, and if his passions are too strong and he feels he ought to marry, he should do as he wants. He is not sinning. They should get married. But the man who has settled the matter in his own mind, who is under no compulsion but has control over his own will, and who has made up his mind not to marry the virgin—this man also does the right thing.

Regarding the man who wants to marry the virgin,[133] Paul lists a series of factors which feed into that decision: worrying that he "might not be acting honourably toward" her, that "his passions are too strong" and that "he feels he ought to".[134] This reinforces the fact that personal preferences are not somehow loosed off from rational deliberation and weighing of multiple factors. Nevertheless, Paul then affirms this man's decision saying "he should do as he wants". Paul does not judge that these factors necessarily bind the man to marry, but rather as justifiable reasons for him to want to.[135]

133 There are several possible reconstructions of the exact scenario Paul has in mind here, but I won't go into that because it is not relevant to the point of my argument.

134 Or possibly she is "past marriageable age", see for example the Holman Christian Standard Bible.

135 The Greek word here can have a range of meanings, including to 'will' or to 'resolve' as well as to 'wish', to 'desire' and 'to want'. This spread of meaning reminds us that we should not begin with assuming too strong a divide between 'will' and 'desire'. See *A Greek-English Lexicon of the New Testament and Other Early Christian Literature,* 3rd edn, rev. and ed. Frederick William Danker, University of Chicago, Chicago, 2000, pp. 447-8.

Regarding the man who does not want to marry, Paul uses several overlapping expressions to safeguard his freedom in this matter: he must have "settled the matter in his own mind", he must be "under no compulsion", he must have "control over his own will" and his mind must be "made up". This repetition urges godly thinking, to ensure that he is not led astray by deceitful desires or the coercion of others. The repetition also reinforces his freedom to choose, for he is not under a moral obligation to act in one way or the other. It is finally his choice to act in this way or that: whether we call this an inclination of will, a movement of his affections, or a resolute desire.

A spiritually formed desire is a good thing. It's not that we do all the thinking, and then after that is finished, we then pay attention to our desires to provide some extra information. Our desires are not another source of moral knowledge. Rather, our reflecting and deliberating is unavoidably shaped by our desires and rightly takes them into account. Thomas Aquinas quotes Aristotle as saying "choice… [can be defined equally well as] either 'intellect influenced by appetite or appetite influenced by intellect'".[136] Choice involves both intellect and desire.

We do need to be suspicious of the deceitfulness of our desires, and so search the motives of our hearts for corrupt schemes, and question our reasoning for self-serving justifications. Hearing God's word is crucial in this:

> For the word of God is alive and active. Sharper than any double-edged sword, it penetrates even to dividing

---

136 Thomas Aquinas, *Summa Theologiae*, part I-II, question 13 'Whether choice is an act of will of reason?' Accessed from *New Advent* (viewed 31 October 2017): www.newadvent.org/summa/2013.htm

　　　　THE GOOD LIFE IN THE LAST DAYS

soul and spirit, joints and marrow; it judges the thoughts and attitudes of the heart. Nothing in all creation is hidden from God's sight. Everything is uncovered and laid bare before the eyes of him to whom we must give account. (Heb 4:12-13)

There is a reason the New Testament speaks about our passions and desires as almost entirely negative forces. The sinful nature has a particular way of distorting our desires so powerfully that they even over-rule what we know to be right and true (Rom 7:23; Eph 2:3, 4:17-22). It is only godly desire, directed by the Spirit towards loving God and loving our neighbour, that should be satisfied.

But searching our hearts is not exactly the same as giving an entirely rational account of our every choice. There are millions of little factors that feed into our choosing one thing over another, including our background and personality. Trying to give a full rational explanation of our decisions simplifies the world[137] and removes the way that God might be mysteriously working through all things in our lives. Our desires are drawn to the goodness of things in the world, in ways that our reason might not always be able to articulate. True wisdom recognizes the limits of our ability to give a fully complete account of all the factors in our decisions.

Consider for example the way we sometimes try to justify why we say 'No' to things. The common productivity proverb 'When you say "yes" to something you are saying "no" to something else', points out that we can't say 'Yes' to everything, that everything we agree to do will detract from

---

137 O'Donovan, *Resurrection and Moral Order,* p. 220.

something else. If we say 'Yes' to staying late at work, we are saying 'No' to being home early to help with our family, for example. The proverb can be reversed as well: 'When you say "no" to something you are saying "yes" to something else.' But this is where it gets tricky, because we don't always have a fully rational explanation for each individual 'No'. When we choose not to do something, we may not be fully clear on what the thing is that we are therefore saying 'Yes' to. For example, imagine that I don't want to join the neighbourhood book club I have been invited to, but it's not because I have something else on at the time that the group meets. It's not clear to me what I am saying 'Yes' to, when I say 'No' to this book club. If I reflect long enough I may well find other priorities that explain the reason for my refusal, but it may not be one single, conflicting commitment. It's not that each time we say "I'd rather not", we must have an equally distinct and valuable thing we are saying 'Yes' to instead. Often the thing we are saying 'Yes' to is a whole "life project"[138] of interlocking good things, that just doesn't include the particular thing you are saying 'No' to. Saying 'No' to a book club that doesn't deeply interest me might be saying 'Yes' to having a little bit of extra margin in my life so that I have energy to say 'Yes' to other things down the track, or just be a bit more present in my life as it is.

This emphasis on free personal choice is found in other places in the New Testament too. For example, when Paul writes to the Corinthians about their contribution to helping the poor Christians in Jerusalem (2 Cor 8-9), he also appeals to them at length, with a range of theological and ethical

138 O'Donovan, *Resurrection and Moral Order*, p. 221.

   THE GOOD LIFE IN THE LAST DAYS

arguments, just like in 1 Corinthians 7. And throughout the appeal he preserves their freedom in how much they give:

> I am not commanding you, but I want to test the sincerity of your love by comparing it with the earnestness of others. (2 Cor 8:8)

> And here is my judgement about what is best for you in this matter. Last year you were the first not only to give but also to have the desire to do so. Now finish the work, so that your eager willingness to do it may be matched by your completion of it, according to your means. For if the willingness is there, the gift is acceptable according to what one has, not according to what one does not have. (8:10-12)

> Each of you should give what you have decided in your heart to give, not reluctantly or under compulsion, for God loves a cheerful giver. (9:7)

And when Peter speaks to Christian leaders he talks about the responsibility and glory of the role, but he also emphasizes the importance of desire in Christian leadership:

> To the elders among you, I appeal as a fellow elder and a witness of Christ's sufferings who also will share in the glory to be revealed: Be shepherds of God's flock that is under your care, watching over them—*not because you must, but because you are willing,* as God wants you to be; not pursuing dishonest gain, but *eager to serve;* not lording it over those entrusted to you, but being examples to the flock. And when the Chief Shepherd appears, you will receive the crown of glory that will never fade away. (1 Pet 5:1-4)

For this reason, personal preference is one of the factors we should consider with our 'good judgement' as we make decisions between 'good' and 'better' options. In *Guidance and the Voice of God*, Jensen and Payne give three decision-making case studies: church, work and marriage.[139] It is a curious omission that in none of these case studies do they mention personal preference—as if aesthetic preference and social fit are not worth considering in joining a church; job satisfaction is irrelevant to job choice; and physical attraction and emotional rapport are unimportant in marriage. It is very important that we let go of a naïve, worldly obsession with such things, as if they are the key to happiness. But we ought not throw the baby out with the bathwater. Personal desire has a legitimate place in our choices as Christians. If I can see many practical and strategic reasons to take a certain course of action, but I really don't want to do it, then all things considered, this is still a legitimate reason to do something else instead:

- "Why did you decide to get married rather than stay single?", someone might ask. To which we might give any number of reasons, including, *"Because I decided to serve God in the goodness of married life."*
- "Why didn't you go into paid Christian leadership?" *"I wanted to be a teacher instead."*
- "Why did you marry Drake instead of Mark-Anthony?" *"Because I liked him and thought he was handsome."*
- "Why did you go to Sojourn Fellowship Church instead of Koinonia Communities?" *"Because I just kind of prefer the vibe there."*

---

**139** Jensen and Payne, *Guidance and the Voice of God*, pp. 117-70.

       THE GOOD LIFE IN THE LAST DAYS

## The abuse of freedom

Like any good thing, however, the legitimacy of personal desire can be abused,° and so this truth must be kept in proportion. Personal preferences must be constantly examined by Scripture to make sure they are not sinful in deceptive ways. They must be informed by Scripture so that they are guided by truths about who God is, who we are and what the nature of the time is. Personal preferences must be alert and sensitive to the particular situations and relationships we find ourselves in. The kinds of holy preferences that arise from all these good influences cannot possibly be indulgent and unconcerned about the glory of God and the needs of others. As Calvin warns:

> For there is scarcely any one whose means allow him to live sumptuously, who does not delight in feasting, and dress, and the luxurious grandeur of his house, who wishes not to surpass his neighbour in every kind of delicacy, and does not plume himself amazingly on his splendour. And all these things are defended under the pretext of Christian liberty. They say they are things indifferent: I admit it, provided they are used indifferently. But when they are too eagerly longed for, when they are proudly boasted of, when they are indulged in luxurious profusion, things which otherwise were in themselves lawful are certainly defiled by these vices.[140]

A particular kind of abuse of freedom is found in the New Testament discussion about Christian freedom, Jewish food

140   Calvin, *Institutes*, book III, chapter 19, section 9.

laws and food sacrificed to pagan idols: it is the unloving disregard for the needs of others. God's word teaches us that we should be willing to freely curb the exercise of our freedom so as to not look down on others, cause disharmony, lead others astray or create barriers for evangelism (Rom 14:15-22; 1 Cor 8:9-13, 9:19-23). We are not compelled to take advantage of the full extent of our freedom because true freedom is to reflect and act in line with God's will and purposes. God can paradoxically describe the reality of Christian freedom by saying "you have been set free from sin and have become slaves of God" (Rom 6:22). Not only are we "slaves of God" but we are also "slaves [of others] because of Jesus" (2 Cor 4:5, HCSB). Paul can describe the use of his own freedom this way: "Though I am free and belong to no-one, I have made myself a slave to everyone, to win as many as possible" (1 Cor 9:19). That means that if I can lovingly restrict my freedom in order to bless someone else then this is one of the most noble expressions of true Christian freedom. But if I stand on my rights and refuse to budge for others then I am abusing the freedom I have in Christ.

We can also abuse our freedom by making unilateral decisions that have a major impact on those closest to us. In the final section of this chapter we will consider the need for mutual consent, particularly in decisions affecting married life.


## Mutual consent in married decisions

If you are married then you are not free to exercise your Christian freedom in complete disregard of your partner. You are one flesh with your partner, so your life decisions,

          THE GOOD LIFE IN THE LAST DAYS

including those about living in the light of the end of the world, need to be made together with them. We have seen an example of this in 1 Corinthians 7:5:

> Do not deprive each other except perhaps by mutual consent and for a time, so that you may devote your-selves to prayer. Then come together again so that Satan will not tempt you because of your lack of self-control.

I find it hard to imagine why the Corinthians might think that refraining from sex would help their prayers. Perhaps this is a concession to their spiritual intuitions rather than an endorsement of the practice, something like "If you really think it would help to abstain so that you can pray, by all means you can, but only with a few conditions…"? A parallel passage in the Jewish Mishnah talks about refraining from sex because of a vow or to study the Torah, so perhaps it is this kind of formal, ritual devotion?[141] Whatever the exact motivation and practice, this verse is similar to the way Paul speaks about the advantages of singleness later on in the chapter: "An unmarried woman or virgin is concerned about the Lord's affairs: Her aim is to be devoted to the Lord in both body and spirit" (v. 34). The married Corinthians are wanting all the benefits of singleness and Paul is saying that they can only recapture such benefits "by mutual consent and for a time".

The principle in this passage does not only apply in the case of deciding not to make love so as to be devoted to prayer. Verses 3-4 speak in very general terms about how

141    Mishnah Ketubot 5:6. Accessed from *Sefaria* (viewed 31 October 2017): www.sefaria.org/Mishnah_Ketubot.5.6?lang=bi&with=all&lang2=en

husband and wife belong to one another: as one flesh they now don't have autonomous authority over themselves, but have a duty to their partner. To not use their body for the good of their partner would be to "defraud" them (a literal translation of the word translated "deprive" in verse 5).[142] This same principle could apply more broadly to any depriving of your spouse from the normal duties and benefits of married life. Garland unpacks how the love command is working out in these verses:

> Love is to control all of the Christian's relationships. It does not insist on its own way… does not seek its own advantage… and always seeks to please others… One can extrapolate from this that Paul believes that love should govern the marriage relationship and that spouses should not treat one another as objects for sexual self-gratification. In marriage, one gives up complete self-determination and must seek to please the partner. The sexual relationship in particular requires mutual sensitivity, loyalty, care, and tenderness.[143]

Just as belonging to one another applies to more than just depriving one another of sex, so also the motivation for such depriving might not be concentrated prayer, but something else. It could be other Christian activities such as leading camps, working long hours in ministry activities or going

---

**142**  It is important to remember the context in which Paul is giving this advice: the Corinthians are neglecting their marriages in the mistaken belief that this would make them more spiritual: "It is good for a man not to have sexual relations with a woman" (v. 1). This same tone and emphasis is not necessarily helpful for the challenges of ongoing sexual activity in the life of a married couple, and is definitely not a justification for one partner demanding sexual satisfaction as an obligation.
**143** Garland, *1 Corinthians*, p. 260.

                    THE GOOD LIFE IN THE LAST DAYS

overseas for mission work. In fact, the principle holds good even for those who neglect their husband or wife for the purposes of secular work, as Christopher Ash observes:

> Today as a pastor, perhaps Paul would have expanded on this in terms of the ways in which husbands and wives may effectively deprive their spouses of a lasting sexual relationship by needless overwork, by preoccupation with work, by obsession with pornography, by the failure to make unhurried and uninterrupted time each for the other and in other ways. The applications are numerous and important.[144]

In all such cases the word of God is clear, any "depriving" can only be done firstly "by mutual consent" and secondly "for a time".

It is very important to note how the idea of the husband being the "head" of the wife (1 Cor 11:3; Eph 5:22-32) does not feature here. When I hear 'headship' spoken about it is often applied by giving examples of decision-making—as the head of the marriage, the husband should have some kind of veto power in decision-making. However, in this case Paul does not go there. Instead this whole paragraph is very symmetrical in the way that it speaks of husband and wife and when it comes to making the decision to refrain from making love for a season, the requirement is "mutual consent".[145]

---

144   Ash, *Marriage: Sex in the Service of God*, p. 191.
145   Any teaching of Scripture can be distorted. So here, the principle of "mutual consent" must not be abused so as to hold one's spouse to ransom. This principle relates to decisions that will have a significant impact on both partners of a marriage. A wife doesn't need consent from her husband to participate in roller derby and a husband doesn't need consent from his wife to commit to a major Warhammer campaign, unless such commitments intrude on their other commitments.

When you are married you cannot make unilateral decisions for the cause of the gospel because "the time is short". Your conscientious zeal and sense of calling does not overrule your duty to your husband or wife. The level of your sacrificial lifestyle is influenced by the person you are married to; you do not have authority over your own body, but yield it to your partner. Perhaps this was lacking in the marriage of Leo McGarry and his wife, from the *West Wing* example I used in the introduction? Perhaps he imposed his career on her rather than making such decisions with her by mutual consent? The dialogue could have been very different:

> Leo: This is the most important thing *we'll* ever do. *We* have to do it well.

> Jenny: It's not more important than our marriage.

> Leo: In a sense it is, darling. This is something *we are doing together*. And *for these few years* while *we're* doing this, yes, it is more important than our marriage.

It's still a 'hard saying' and it would still require him to demonstrate genuine affection and partnership in a million small and large ways over time. But this sense of shared enterprise definitely takes the hateful tone out of the exchange.

A few years ago a friend of a friend shared their experience of being the wife of a US serviceman. The description beautifully captures this sense of shared mission:

> I don't feel neglected, because he makes me feel like I am doing a very important job. We just moved to Korea. He went away for a week and he had several things that he needed me to do for him here—

appointments, moving our stuff into our new house, signing the lease, etc. It was a challenge, and I felt like an important part of the team. I was proud to show him all I'd done when he got home. We both ask each other how our day was, and he hopes I am making friends here. We have lots of friends at church, and some here at my apartment too. I've gotten a chance to meet some military wives here, and I knew quite a few while I was in the military, either personally, or through their husbands with whom I served.

...The impression I get of military wives is that they are very proud of the service their husbands do. The serviceman's family is really respected by the military. They get to come on base and use all the facilities even when the husband is away. They are honoured at military functions. There are lots of activities to include them. They don't feel bitter or neglected usually because they are practically part of the military. They also have a lot of support from other women, but just like anything else, it depends who you spend your time with whether they will support your husband or gossip and try to create enmity in your family.

Yes, the family really consider themselves part of the military—if he is serving, we are too. The whole family makes a sacrifice, the whole family serves their country, whether we are travelling overseas together, moving across country, or just having to wait at home while he deploys. But the same way you'll see videos of the Marines out in the desert dancing, singing, joking around—most families keep the pride and sacrifice in their back pocket for the tough times and official functions. They have the confidence of knowing it, but don't dwell on it all the time, because they don't want to always be worrying about their husband's safety, or drawing attention to themselves. Many say "it's in God's hands." I think military families who have faith in God stay together more and are more positive.

Some women don't ever want their husbands to get out of the military, they like it so much (some women also marry military men for the money, the independence, but that's a whole other story). Some want their husband out of the military ASAP. It just depends on the person. Women who love their husbands don't like them being gone all the time, but are happy if their husband is happy. So if he likes being in the military, I want him to stay in, even though I know it could be hard for us. Someone has got to defend the country, and as long as he wants to be that someone, I will do my best to support his service from home.

When married, your decisions around how exactly you 'live as if' must be made with mutual consent.


## Holy flexibility in decision-making

When it comes to decision-making, in many areas our intuition is to say that 'Oh that's a wisdom issue', meaning 'there's no one right way'. In this final chapter I have shown from 1 Corinthians 7 that this intuition is actually supported by the biblical evidence. It is God's will that his people be free to make a range of different godly decisions in obedience to his word. Christians are genuinely free to choose among multiple good things. We are free to wisely deliberate and then act in line with our choices made in wisdom and shaped by love for God and neighbour. We are even free to choose what might appear to be the less-than-best option, or the less strategic thing. We are free in some decisions for our personal desires, informed by the word of God and shaped by a godly character, to be the deciding factor. Allowing for flexibility is not simply a way that we shrug our shoulders and keep the peace, as if there really is one way to live but we have decided to graciously resign ourselves to substandard performance because of our fallen human weakness. It is glorifying to God when his people wisely think things through and exercise their godly freedom to do what they want.

This diversity of action, in our Lord's providence, produces all sorts of great outcomes that would not otherwise come about. The Christians who remain in the work force rather than going into paid Christian ministry are connected with many non-Christian people, and given the opportunity to do unique good deeds because of their jobs. Christians who buy nice things are able to freely share them with others, including the church. Those who earn a lot have the ability to give, not only to the church but also to charitable and parachurch organisations. Those who invest significant amounts into sport or hobbies find themselves networked with non-Christians they might have otherwise never met. Don't misunderstand me, I am not saying that these kinds of outcomes are the justification for the decision. It can be a wretched business when Christians seek to explain their every decision through the speculative ways that it will actually prove to be 'good for the kingdom'. This is often a sign that we are not acting in true freedom of conscience, but rather trying to calm some underlying guilt, or guard against the judgement of others. While it is right to examine our hearts and consider all the pros and cons of various decisions, my point here is that all sorts of good things can come about as a wonderful by-product of our peculiar choices.

This same Christian freedom also gives rise to extraordinary acts of radical sacrifice. A Christian gives up a career with great pay and high cultural capital in order to become an evangelist among university students. A family makes significant changes to their consumption, lifestyle habits, holiday expectations and educational and extra-curricular choices in order to give enormous amounts away to gospel ministry and those in need. Another Christian has their entire life shaped and constrained by deep and ongoing investment in the lives of vulnerable and needy people. The wonderful truth of the power of the Spirit as he applies the gospel to our hearts and minds is that such decisions as these can and do come, not out of guilty compulsion or extremely specific preaching applications, but out of the free response to the grace of God in Christ.

# CONCLUSION

Why did I bother to write this particular book? What is the intended outcome of a book like this? What is my prayer for you, my readers, as you digest what I have had to say and weigh it up against God's word and your lives?

*For the strong and sacrificial* it is my hope that you continue to use your abilities and energy wholeheartedly for the kingdom of God, while not imposing your particular expression of devotion to God and response to the reality of the last days on others. I hope this book helps you separate out your free decisions from gospel imperatives. I also pray that the book might help prepare you for the difficult occasion where some of you might "hit the wall" in life and ministry. Can you carry on serving Christ in good conscience when the zeal is burning low?

*For the bruised reed,* who has been ground down by the trials of life, or burned out by your own unrestrained zeal, or used up by the thoughtless drive of others who have dragged you along: I hope you have heard me distance myself from a foolish, inhumane and inflexible approach to the sacrificial Christian life. I don't want to be another accusing finger pointing at you. I hope I have put into words some of your own concerns and insights. My prayer is that I might be able to give the Bible back to you, so that you can hear the hard sayings of Scripture in a better light, not as suffocating and destructive words that make you flinch. And my hope is that I might be able to give your zealous fellow believers back to you, that you might genuinely rejoice in their zeal and sacrifice, even as you might give them wise words of caution.

*For the preacher and teacher and friend,* I want to urge you to be careful as you exhort and advise. Every church community will have its normal way of conducting Sunday gatherings and living life together. Cultural norms are not only unavoidable but actually helpful to us. But we must be careful that we don't turn helpful principles into binding laws. As Calvin warns, "we must always attend to the exception, that they must not be thought necessary to salvation, nor lay the conscience under a religious obligation; they must not be compared to the worship of God, nor substituted for piety".[146] Living in 'gospel communities', or defining key steps to moving people along a discipleship pathway, or other similar patterns and standards are unavoidable in church life. But they are only ever proxies of genuine spirituality.

*For the confused and deflated,* who sense that life is complicated, and realize you have to be flexible to the needs of others and trust your doctor when they tell you to look after your wellbeing… but deep down worry that you have compromised on true Christian zeal. I have tried to show that your growing sense that it's complicated is in fact biblical. Your intuitions about a need for wisdom, realism and flexibility are true, and they are explicitly reflected in

---

**146** Calvin, *Institutes,* book IV, chapter 11, section 27.

the pages of Scripture. May this discovery free you from a sneaking suspicion that you have really lost touch with real Christianity.

In doing all this I hope to add more energy to the individual Christian, to whole churches and to networks of churches. So much spiritual zeal can be absorbed in anxiety about whether we are being 'full-on' enough and so serving out of a strained, driven, earnestness. So much goodwill in the church community is smothered by a severe discernment, seeking to squash square-shaped people and octagonal-shaped people into one round hole. How much better if our zeal can be fanned into flames through grace, joy and freedom? I pray that as grace rules the church in wisdom there will be joyous enthusiasm and rich diversity that will be used by our Lord to spread the gospel and build the church to his glory.

How then do we live in these last days? We put God first and die to our sinful selves. We serve God in the diversity of his world. Guided by God's word we wisely treat things as they are, where they are and when they are—and do all this knowing who we ourselves are. We treat all the good things in this world as relative goods because this world is passing away but we trust that living this way is the best life we could live. And we make decisions in the light of all of this with realism, recognizing diversity, being content, thinking it through under the word of God and doing what we want.

# ABOUT MIKEY LYNCH

Mikey graduated from the University of Tasmania with a Bachelor of Arts in 2002. In 2000 he became one of the founding leaders of Crossroads Presbyterian Church where he was the lead pastor for seven years from 2003.

Mikey now works as the Campus Director of the University Fellowship of Christians, University of Tasmania, Hobart. Mikey is the chairman of The Vision 100 Network (Tasmania) and a founding director of Geneva Push (national)—both church planting networks. He is also a chaplain at Jane Franklin Hall.

Mikey's ministry has focused on preaching to unchurched university students and graduates. He is also passionate about identifying and developing future Christian leaders. Mikey is married to Nikki and is the father of Xavier, Esther and Toby. He loves cooking, fishing, reading and has recently taken up rollerblading again.

Matthias Media is an evangelical publishing ministry that seeks to persuade all Christians of the truth of God's purposes in Jesus Christ as revealed in the Bible, and equip them with high-quality resources, so that by the work of the Holy Spirit they will:

- abandon their lives to the honour and service of Christ in daily holiness and decision-making
- pray constantly in Christ's name for the fruitfulness and growth of his gospel
- speak the Bible's life-changing word whenever and however they can— in the home, in the world and in the fellowship of his people.

Our resources range from Bible studies and books through to training courses, audio sermons and children's Sunday School material. To find out more, and to access samples and free downloads, visit our website:

# www.matthiasmedia.com

## How to buy our resources

1. Direct from us over the internet:
    – in the US: www.matthiasmedia.com
    – in Australia: www.matthiasmedia.com.au

2. Direct from us by phone: please visit our website for current phone contact information.

3. Through a range of outlets in various parts of the world. Visit **www.matthiasmedia.com/contact** for details about recommended retailers in your part of the world.

4. Trade enquiries can be addressed to:
    – in the US and Canada: sales@matthiasmedia.com
    – in Australia and the rest of the world: sales@matthiasmedia.com.au

Register at our website for our **free** regular email update to receive information about the latest new resources, **exclusive special offers**, and free articles to help you grow in your Christian life and ministry.